ON THE TRAIL OF ARTHUR CONAN DOYLE

ON THE TRAIL OF ARTHUR CONAN DOYLE:

An Illustrated Devon Tour

Brian W Pugh and Paul R Spiring

Book Guild Publishing
Sussex, England

First published in Great Britain in 2008 by
The Book Guild Ltd
Pavilion View
19 New Road
Brighton, BN1 1UF

Typesetting in Garamond by
Acorn Bookwork Ltd, Salisbury, Wiltshire

Printed in Great Britain by
CPI Antony Rowe

A catalogue record for this book is available from
The British Library.

ISBN 978 1 84624 198 7

Dedication

The authors would like to thank their respective partners and family for instructing them to finish this book! They would also like to thank their friends in The Conan Doyle (Crowborough) Establishment and at the European School of Karlsruhe for their continued support.

Contents

Foreword

Arthur Conan Doyle led a remarkably varied and exciting life, the sort that you might associate with an out-and-out eccentric – which he was not. He was, however, versatile, courageous, intelligent, dedicated and open-minded. There have been many biographies, and you might think that every aspect of his life had been covered, yet new information is constantly being unearthed, as this book shows.

The name of Arthur Conan Doyle has long been overshadowed by that of his most famous creation, Sherlock Holmes. Probably most people, if you mention Dartmoor, will think of Holmes's greatest adventure, *The Hound of the Baskervilles*. But Conan Doyle's connections with Dartmoor, and with Devon generally, reach far beyond this one book. His first practice after qualifying as a physician was in Plymouth. It was a short-lived engagement, but Dr Conan Doyle returned to the county on many occasions.

The lives of two other men are inextricably bound up with Conan Doyle's experiences in Devon: George Turnavine Budd, who took him on as a partner at the Plymouth practice, and Bertram Fletcher Robinson, who played an essential part in conceiving and planning *The Hound of the Baskervilles*. The contributions of both are fully and fairly dealt with in this book.

Others have provided guides for those romantic souls who wish to follow the trail of Sherlock Holmes. I am delighted to welcome a book that concentrates instead on the detective's creator, and one, moreover, written with the joint authority of the scientist and the Doylean scholar.

Roger Johnson,
Editor: *The Sherlock Holmes Journal.*

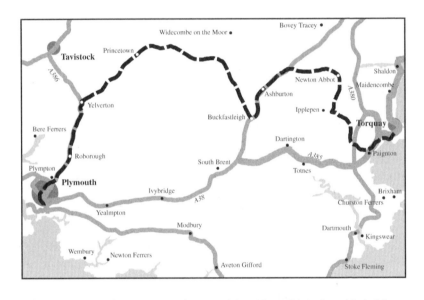

Plate 1. The Arthur Conan Doyle Devon Tour (the trail is indicated in bold).

Preface

Between 1882 and 1923, Arthur Conan Doyle, the creator of the legendary character of Sherlock Holmes, visited Devon on no fewer than ten separate occasions and resided for some four months in total. This book aims to set these visits within the wider context of his life and enable readers to retrace some of his footsteps across the county for themselves. It is designed to appeal to readers irrespective of their knowledge about either the life or works of Conan Doyle.

This book is in two parts. The first part (Chapters 1–3) will introduce the reader to the three major subjects, Sir Arthur Conan Doyle, Dr George Turnavine Budd and Bertram Fletcher Robinson. The second part (Chapter 4) will enable the reader to tour the non-fictional sites in Devon with which these major protagonists were most closely associated. Please note that places marked with an asterisk in Chapter 4 are private property and visitors are requested to respect the privacy of any tenants.

The full tour is a semi-circular route which incorporates 18 locations and 36 points of interest (see Plate 1 and Chapter 4). Visitors must drive 59.2 miles along various classifications of road and walk 1.5 miles along mainly flat footpaths. The suggested tour begins in Plymouth and ends at Torquay; it encompasses Roborough, Princetown, Buckfastleigh, Ashburton, Newton Abbot, Ipplepen and Paignton respectively. Alternatively, readers might choose to reverse the tour or undertake a partial and more localised section of it.

For refreshments en route, the following are recommended: Strand Tea Rooms (24 New Street, The Barbican, Plymouth), Valentis Cafe Bar (The Promenade, The Hoe, Plymouth), The Lopes Arms (Tavistock Road, Roborough), Fox Tor Cafe (Two Bridges Road, Princetown), The Forest Inn (Hexworthy), The

Old Coffee House (West Street, Ashburton) and Compass Bar and Lounge (The Grand Hotel, Torbay Road, Torquay). There are also many hotels, inns and places offering bed and breakfast accommodation located along the way.

Happy touring!

Brian Pugh and Paul Spiring

Acknowledgements

The authors would like to thank the following for their assistance with this book: Ann Adams (Budd family), Ashburton Library, Peter Basham (Royal College of Physicians of London), Phillip G. Bergem (Norwegian Explorers), Michael Bourne (Baskerville family), Bob Brewis (Historian to Freemason Torbay Lodge No. 1358), Bristol Central Library (Reference), Bristol Record Office, Cambridge University Library (Rare Books and Periodicals), Graeme de Bracey Marrs (Robinson family), Devon Record Office, Shelah Duncan (The British Library), Simon Eliot (Headmaster of Sherborne School), Exeter Central Library (Westcountry Studies), Michael Freeland (Harold Michelmore & Company Solicitors, Newton Abbot), Irene Ferguson (Assistant Archivist at Edinburgh University), Laxmi Gadher (Record Copying Department of The National Archive, Richmond), General Register Office, John Genova, Stewart Gillies (The British Library), Annabel Gordon (TopFoto), Freda Howlett (President of The Sherlock Holmes Society of London), Ipplepen Library, Roger Johnson (Editor of The Sherlock Holmes Journal), Tim Johnson (The Sherlock Holmes Collection, The University of Minnesota), Liverpool Central Library and Archive, Pat Luxford (Ford Park Cemetery Trust), Ian MacGregor (Archive Information Manager for the Met Office, Exeter), Janice McNabb, Meade-King, Robinson and Company Limited (Liverpool), Newton Abbot Library (Local Studies and Railway Studies), Peggy Perdue (The Friends of the Arthur Conan Doyle Collection, Toronto Public Library, Canada), Plymouth and West Devon Record Office, Plymouth Central Library (Local and Naval Studies), Mark Pool (Torquay Library), Harry Rabbich, Christopher Redmond, John Richardson (Headmaster of Cheltenham College), Arthur Robinson (Robinson family),

Mark Steed (Headmaster of Kelly College, Tavistock), Brian and Maggie Sutton, Troy Taylor (Illinois Hauntings Tour Company), The Society for Psychical Research (London), Philip Weller and Jane Weller (The Baskerville Hounds, The Dartmoor Sherlock Holmes Study Group and The Conan Doyle Study Group), Frances Willmoth (Archivist at Jesus College, Cambridge University), Doug Wrigglesworth (The Friends of the Arthur Conan Doyle Collection, Toronto Public Library, Canada) and especially Patrick Casey (Clifton Rugby Club).

Chapter One

Sir Arthur Conan Doyle
(22nd May 1859 – 7th July 1930)

Plate 2. Sir Arthur Conan Doyle.

Introduction

Arthur Ignatius Conan Doyle (hereinafter ACD) was born 22nd May 1859 (see Plate 2). He was the son of an artist and architect called Charles Altamont Doyle and Mary Josephine Doyle (née Foley) of 11 Picardy Place, Edinburgh. ACD was baptised into the

1

Roman Catholic religion and given the name Conan in order to perpetuate that of his childless godfather and great uncle, Michael Conan. ACD was one of nine children: Annette (b. 1856), Catherine (b. 1858), Arthur (b. 1859), Mary (b. 1861) Caroline (b. 1866), Constance (b. 1868), John (b. 1873), Jane (b. 1875) and Bryan Mary (b. 1877).

ACD was initially educated at the Newington Academy, Edinburgh. At the age of eight years he was sent to the Jesuit preparatory school called Hodder in Lancashire. Two years later he was admitted to nearby Stonyhurst College. At the age of 16 ACD left Stonyhurst and continued his education for one more year at a sister school called Stella Matutina at Feldkirch in Austria. On his return home to Scotland, ACD stopped in Paris to spend some weeks with Michael Conan, who urged him to consider a medical career. Upon his arrival in Edinburgh, ACD found that it had been predetermined that he should study medicine and not the arts, a decision probably arrived at under the influence of a family friend and physician called Bryan Charles Waller, who boarded with the Doyle family at this time.

The Early Medical Years

It has been widely reported that ACD entered Edinburgh University Medical School during October 1876 (Waller's Alma Mater). However, a note written on 17th May 1882 by one Thomas Gilbert, the then 'Clerk to Edinburgh University', reports that ACD actually commenced his medical studies on 1st November 1877. In any event, during his time as a student, ACD was taught by Dr Joseph Bell, upon whom the character Sherlock Holmes was largely based. He also met Professor William Rutherford, who was the model for a later fictional character, Professor George Edward Challenger.

During June 1879, ACD began working as a medical assistant to one Dr Reginald Hoare in Birmingham. In October of that same year, ACD returned to Edinburgh and befriended a final-year medical student called George Turnavine Budd (see Chapter 2). In January 1880, ACD attended a lecture in Birmingham that was entitled *Does Death end all?* He professed to have found the subject interesting but unconvincing. Nevertheless, ACD maintained a life-long interest in psychical phenomena from then on.

In late February 1880, ACD began working as an unqualified surgeon aboard a whaling ship called *Hope* that was destined for the Arctic Circle. He was paid a flat rate of two pounds and ten shillings per month, plus an additional three shillings for every ton of whale oil collected. During this voyage ACD fell from the ice into a freezing sea and narrowly avoided drowning by using a skinned seal carcass to haul himself out. On 10th August of that same year, ACD returned to Scotland and thereafter, rejoined Dr Hoare in Birmingham.

On 1st August 1881, ACD was awarded both a first class Bachelors degree in Medicine and a Masters degree in Surgery from Edinburgh University. In October of that same year, he was employed as a surgeon aboard a cargo steamer called *Mayumba* that was bound for West Africa. During this trip he contracted typhoid and almost died. On 14th January 1882, ACD returned to Liverpool and shortly afterwards, he rejoined Dr Hoare in Birmingham for one final time. In early May of that same year, he became the junior medical partner to George Turnavine Budd in the East Stonehouse district of what is now Plymouth (see Chapter 2).

During June 1882, ACD took a trip from Plymouth to Tavistock stopping en route at Roborough. This excursion inspired him to write an article entitled *Dry Plates on a Wet Moor* that was published in *The British Journal of Photographs* in November 1882. The 'genius' referred to in this article is probably George Turnavine Budd, who also appears very thinly disguised in a short story entitled *Crabbe's Practice* (1884). In 1892, ACD wrote a Sherlock Holmes story entitled *Silver Blaze* that is set about Tavistock.

ACD used Budd as the model for a character called Dr James Cullingworth in two books entitled *The Stark Munro Letters* (1895) and *Memories and Adventures* (1924).

Plate 3. ACD at his Southsea medical practice.
THE TROY TAYLOR COLLECTION.

During June 1882, ACD and Budd dissolved their partnership. Thereafter, ACD decided to leave Plymouth for Portsmouth in Hampshire, armed with only £10 in his pocket and a 'devil-may-care optimism of youth as to the future'. By early July of that same year, he had opened a practice in nearby Southsea at 1, Bush Villas, Elm Grove (see Plate 3). However, business was slow at first and ACD later recalled that there 'was a grocer who developed epileptic fits, which meant butter and tea for me'. Nevertheless, over the eight years that he worked in Southsea, ACD became a reasonably successful physician and earned as much as £300 a year. He was also elected assistant honorary secretary of Portsmouth Literary and Scientific Society and played goalkeeper

Plate 4. Louisa 'Touie' Hawkins.
THE TROY TAYLOR COLLECTION.

and full-back for Portsmouth Football Club under the assumed name of A. C. Black.

During early 1885, ACD treated a 25-year-old patient called John Hawkins, affectionately referred to as 'Jack' by his family. John was suffering from the then incurable disease of bacterial meningitis and had been taken to see ACD by his elder sister, Louisa Hawkins (see Plate 4). At this time, society would frequently ostracise sufferers because the cause of their alarming convulsive fits was not understood. Nevertheless, ACD installed John in his own home and personally nursed him until his death on 25th March 1885.

Louisa (b. 10th April 1857) preferred to be addresssed as 'Louise' and perhaps for that reason, she was also nicknamed 'Touie'. Louise was 27 years old and a 'a very feminine home-loving girl of great gentleness and complete unselfishness'. ACD and Louise married on 1st August 1885, just five days after he was awarded a Doctorate of Medicine by Edinburgh University. The wedding was held at Thornton-in-Lonsdale in Yorkshire and Dr Bryan Charles Waller acted as best man. Later, ACD wrote of Louise that 'no man could have had a more gentle and amiable life's companion'.

During 1886, ACD wrote *A Study in Scarlet*, in which he introduced his legendary detective, Sherlock Holmes. This story was first published during 1887 in *Beeton's Christmas Annual* and later republished in book form by Ward, Lock & Company Limited of London (1888). Interestingly, ACD had initially intended to call this story *A Tangled Skein* and use two principal characters with the names of Sherrinford Holmes and Ormond Sacker. However, feeling these were rather awkward, he changed them to Sherlock Holmes and Dr John Watson. Watson probably derived his name from one Dr James Watson, who on 26th January 1887, had attended ACD's initiation as a Freemason at Portsmouth Lodge No. 257.

On 28th January 1889, Louise Conan Doyle gave birth to their first child, a daughter called Mary Louise Conan Doyle. During August of this same year, ACD attended a literary soirée in London, hosted by an American editor, Joseph Stoddart, who wished to recruit British writers for his magazine. As a direct result, ACD wrote a second Holmes story entitled *The Sign of Four* that was first published in the February 1890 edition of *Lippincott's Magazine* (Philadelphia).

In 1891, ACD left Southsea and travelled to Vienna with the intention of studying eye medicine. However, this plan fell through so he relocated to London and opened his own surgery instead. Business was slow, so ACD soon abandoned medicine altogether in favour of writing.

'Arise, Sir Arthur!'

In January 1891, George Newnes MP founded a magazine called *The Strand Magazine* (edited by Herbert Greenhough Smith until

1930). Newnes had previously founded *The Westminster Gazette* (1873), *Tit-Bits* (1881) and *The Wide World Magazine* (1888). It is interesting to note that Newnes published many of the Sherlock Holmes stories written by ACD after 1891 and that he had close links to Devon. For example, in 1887 Newnes financed the construction of an innovative cliff railway that still interconnects Lynton and Lynmouth and that works on a water counter-balance principle (opened Easter Monday 1890). He also obtained an Act of Parliament that enabled construction of the Lynton and Barnstaple Railway (opened 1898). Later, Newnes financed the construction of Lynton Town Hall that bears him a commemorative stone and bust dedication (opened 14th August 1900). On 9th June 1910 Baronet George Newnes JP, died aged 51 years at his mansion called Hollerday House in Lynton. He is buried nearby at 'The Old Cemetery' close to The Valley of Rocks. On August 4th 1913, an empty Hollerday House was destroyed by a fire allegedly set by Suffragists (it was demolished shortly after WWII).

During July 1891, *The Strand Magazine* published a Sherlock Holmes adventure entitled *A Scandal in Bohemia*. This proved so successful that ACD was commissioned to write a further eleven Sherlock Holmes short stories that were each published in *The Strand Magazine* between August 1891 and June 1892. In October 1892, all twelve of these were republished in book form as *The Adventures of Sherlock Holmes* (London: George Newnes). Each was illustrated by an artist called Sidney Paget and ACD was paid between £35 and £50 per story. However, by November 1891, ACD was already weary of Sherlock Holmes and remarked in a letter to his mother that he was contemplating 'slaying Holmes in the last and winding him up for good and all'.

During February 1892, ACD was offered £1,000 to write a second series of Sherlock Holmes stories for *The Strand Magazine*. Later the same year, ACD travelled with his family to Norway where he skied for the first time. Upon their return to England, Louise was diagnosed as suffering from tuberculosis and given only a few months to live. ACD then took his wife to Davos in

Switzerland where it was felt that the climate might relieve her symptoms. On 15th November 1892, despite her illness, Louise gave birth to a healthy son, Arthur Alleyne Kingsley Conan Doyle (affectionately referred to as 'Kingsley').

On 16th December 1892, ACD attended a dinner at the Reform Club in Pall Mall. This dinner was held to celebrate the pending publication of the 100th edition of the Cambridge University undergraduate periodical, *The Granta*. ACD sat next to a fellow Reform Club member called John Robinson who was manager of *The Daily News* and also an uncle of Bertram Fletcher Robinson (see Chapter 3). Both men were friends of a fellow guest and club member, Thomas Wemyss Reid, editor of the *Leeds Mercury*, a newspaper referred to by Sherlock Holmes in *The Hound of the Baskervilles* (London: George Newnes, 1902).

In December 1893, ACD 'killed-off' Sherlock Holmes at the Reichenbach Falls in Switzerland in a story called *The Final Problem*, which concluded the second series of tales in *The Strand Magazine*. During that same month, this serialisation was republished in a book entitled *The Memoirs of Sherlock Holmes* (London: George Newnes).

Between 2nd October and 8th December 1894, ACD toured North America with his younger brother, John Francis Innes Hay Doyle (referred to as 'Innes' by friends and family). On 3rd November 1894, ACD wrote to John Robinson from Amherst House, Amherst, Massachusetts. Robinson had recently been knighted and elected to the committee of the Reform Club. In his letter ACD discussed the first five weeks of his first North America lecture-tour and detailed the arrangements for his return to England. He begins thus:

MY DEAR ROBINSON

May I make you my mouth-piece in conveying my warm remembrances to friends of the Reform, above all to Payn and Reid?

It is interesting to note that ACD seldom addressed his friends by their Christian names. This same formal greeting was later used in two acknowledgements published in the first book editions of *The Hound of the Baskervilles* (see Chapter 3).

ACD returned to England on 15th December 1894. Shortly afterwards, *The Strand Magazine* published the first in a series of short stories by ACD featuring a new hero called Brigadier Etienne Gerard.

During 1895, the author Grant Allen suggested to ACD that the air in Surrey might be beneficial to the health of Louise. ACD subsequently purchased a plot of land in Hindhead and commissioned his architect friend, Joseph Henry Ball, to design a house. It was completed by October 1897 and named Undershaw.

Throughout the summer of 1895, ACD and Louise holidayed in Switzerland. They then decided to winter in Egypt and arrived there in November of that same year. In January 1896, ACD had the first of a twelve-part serialisation entitled *Rodney Stone* published in *The Strand Magazine*. In that same month, ACD and Louise embarked upon a Nile cruise between Egypt and Sudan. During this trip, ACD reported on hostilities between the British Army and Dervishes for *The Westminster Gazette*. This experience inspired his dramatic desert story *The Tragedy of the Korosko* that was published in *The Strand Magazine* between May and December 1897. ACD and Louise returned to Hindhead in April 1896, but Undershaw was not completed. Consequently, they first rented a property called Grayswood Beeches in Haslemere and then relocated to the nearby Moorlands Hotel.

Between 8th January and 5th March 1897, ACD's novel *Uncle Bernac* was serialised in *The Manchester Weekly Times*. During February of the same year, ACD travelled to Devon to meet the family of a woman whom his 23-year-old brother Innes was interested in marrying. The girl in question was probably 20-year-old Dora G. Hamilton who resided with her parents and a large staff of servants at Retreat Mansion in Topsham (now part of Exeter). Dora's father was Alexander Hamilton, a prominent landowner. In the event, no wedding took place and Innes later married Clara Schwensen, a Danish woman, on 2nd August 1911.

On 15th March 1897, 37-year-old ACD attended a party in London and met the woman who was to become his second wife, Jean Elizabeth Leckie (see Plate 5). Jean was the 23-year-old daughter (b. 14th March 1874) of a Scottish family who were then living at Blackheath in Kent. She was well-read, a skilled horse-woman and a trained opera singer. It was a genuine love-match but ACD continued to nurse and cherish Louise until her death in 1906. ACD's family and friends were naturally divided on the subject of Jean Leckie but some accepted her into their circle.

During October 1899, the Second Boer War (1899–1902) began in South Africa and ACD attempted to enlist in the

Plate 5. Jean Leckie.
THE TROY TAYLOR COLLECTION.

Middlesex Yeomanry. However, the military authorities rejected him because of his age and condition. In spite of this set-back, during late February 1900, ACD sailed to South Africa in order to take up a voluntary position as a physician at the Langman Hospital in Bloemfontein. During his service there, he contracted dysentery and also experienced a recurrence of typhoid fever. In July of that same year, a weakened ACD returned to England in the company of Bertram Fletcher Robinson aboard the SS *Briton*.

During August 1900, ACD played for the Marylebone Cricket Club (M.C.C.) against London County at Crystal Palace in London. During this game he recorded his only first-class wicket when he dismissed the famous Bristol born cricketer, William Gilbert 'WG' Grace (then aged 52 years).

In October 1900, ACD was defeated as the Conservative and Liberal Unionist parliamentary candidate for Edinburgh Central. Later that same month, Smith, Elder & Company published *The Great Boer War*, a book that ACD constantly updated. When the war concluded in 1902, this book had run to at least 16 editions.

On 31st March 1901, Louise and her mother, Emily Hawkins, stayed at Bolton's Boarding House, Tor Church Road, Torquay, Meanwhile, ACD was staying with his mother and Jean Leckie at the Ashdown Forest Hotel in Forest Row near East Grinstead in Sussex. ACD's two children, twelve-year-old Mary and eight-year-old Kingsley, remained at Undershaw with their spinster aunt who was also called Emily Hawkins (affectionately referred to as 'Nem').

On 26th April 1901, ACD and Bertram Fletcher Robinson took a three-day golfing holiday at the Royal Links Hotel in Cromer, Norfolk. Four weeks later, the two men visited Dartmoor together and stayed at Rowe's Duchy Hotel in Princetown. By September 1901, ACD had written *The Hound of the Baskervilles*, thereby 'resurrecting' Sherlock Holmes. This largely Devon-based story has formed the basis of at least 19 full-length films and many more television adaptations (see Chapter 3).

On 16th January 1902, ACD's views about the Second Boer War were published in a sixpenny pamphlet entitled *The War in*

South Africa – Its Cause and Conduct. This work was probably prompted by the growing public unease at home about foreign reports of alleged British atrocities and the use of concentration camps. ACD did not condone the conditions in the British camps, but he argued that there was a need to isolate guerrilla Boers from the homestead families who supported their activities. Such defence of British policy in layman's terms won him unprecedented public acclaim. The pamphlet was translated into numerous languages and sold in record numbers; ACD donated the revenue it generated to various good causes, including a reconciliation fund for disadvantaged Boers. The Second Boer War ended in May that year with the signing of the Treaty of Vereeniging.

Around August 1902, ACD secured a job for Jean Leckie's 20-year-old brother, Robert, at 'Newnes' office'. That same month, he played several cricket matches at Teignmouth in South Devon. About that same time, Jean and her mother, Selina, travelled to Teignmouth from North Devon where they had been holidaying. On 16th August 1902, ACD wrote to his mother and stated that he intended to meet Jean at Newton Abbot on 23rd August. He added that they would drive 'over some of the Baskerville Moor Country' and that 'it will be charming'. Thereafter, ACD also met Jean in nearby Exeter and they saw the barracks where Innes had once resided. In early September, ACD visited Lynton, the location of George Newnes' home. Whilst there, he planned to hunt with the Devon Stag Hounds on Exmoor.

On 24th October 1902, ACD was both knighted ('Knights Bachelor') and appointed a Deputy Lieutenant of Surrey by Edward VII at Buckingham Palace. Officially, ACD was honoured for services to his country during the Second Boer War. However, it is interesting to note that Edward VII was reportedly an avid Sherlock Holmes fan and that he had also attended a gala performance of William Gillette's play, *Sherlock Holmes*, on 1st February 1902 at The Lyceum Theatre in London.

In 1903, ACD travelled to Birmingham and purchased a ten-horse power Wolseley motorcar. After very little training in its operation, he then elected to drive 150 miles back to Undershaw. During May of that same year, the second series of the *Brigadier Gerard* stories was concluded in *The Strand Magazine*. Meanwhile, ACD had reluctantly agreed to continue the revival of Sherlock Holmes and he subsequently wrote a further 13 short stories that each appeared in *The Strand Magazine* between October 1903 and December 1904 (illustrated by Sidney Paget). In 1905, these stories were compiled and published as *The Return of Sherlock Holmes* by George Newnes.

Early in 1904, ACD was invited to join a select twelve-man London-based crime club called 'Our Society'. Bertram Fletcher Robinson and Max Pemberton were also elected at the same time (see Chapter 3). On 18th June of that same year, both ACD and Bertram Fletcher Robinson attended a dinner at the Savoy Hotel in London that was held in honour of Lord Roberts. This dinner was hosted by Joseph Hodges Choate, the then American Ambassador to the United Kingdom. The guest list included many British dignitaries, all of whom were members of an Anglo-American society entitled 'The Pilgrims'.

On 7th April 1905, Edinburgh University awarded ACD the honorary degree of Doctorate of Letters. Later that same month, he visited the sites of the notorious Whitechapel Murders committed by 'Jack the Ripper'. ACD was accompanied by Dr Samuel Ingleby Oddie (later His Majesty's Coroner for Central London) and other members of 'Our Society'.

In January 1906, ACD was defeated as the Unionist parliamentary candidate for the Hawick Division of the Scottish Borders. He then returned to Undershaw to focus upon his writing and to be close to Louise, who had been visibly waning for some 18 months. On 4th July of that same year, the first Lady Conan Doyle died aged 49 years. She was buried at Grayshot Church near the family home in Hindhead. ACD was deeply affected by her death and entered into a depression.

On 10th August 1906, ACD visited the Leckie family home,

Monkstown, at Lordswell Lane, Crowborough, Sussex. On 19th October 1906, Max Pemberton delivered a speech to 'Our Society' that was entitled *An Attempt to Blackmail Me*. Just two days later, ACD, Bertram Fletcher Robinson, Innes Doyle and two other friends played golf together at Hindhead in Surrey.

On 7th January 1907, ACD revisited Monkstown. Whilst there, he appears to have fallen in love with a nearby cottage called 'Little Windlesham' that was then owned by one Mrs Scott-Malden (ACD later bought, enlarged and renamed this property). That same month, he began actively campaigning for the release from prison of one George Edalji who had been convicted of cattle maiming during 1903. Consequently, ACD made frequent trips between Undershaw and London to visit the Home Office, Scotland Yard and offices of *The Daily Telegraph*.

On 21st January 1907, ACD's 36-year-old friend, Bertram Fletcher Robinson, died in London. Robinson's funeral service was held three days later at St Andrew's Church, Ipplepen, Devon. A floral tribute was received with a message that read 'In loving memory of an old and valued friend from Arthur Conan Doyle'. Later, ACD lamented that Robinson was 'a fine fellow, whose premature death was a loss to the world'.

A Second Family and Other Interests

During February 1907, ACD wrote to his mother and outlined his provisional thoughts in relation to the arrangements for marrying Jean. The following month, ACD spent several days at Monkstown and was present for Jean's birthday. In May of that same year, George Edalji's conviction for cattle maiming was quashed thanks largely to the efforts of ACD. About that same time, ACD and Jean became officially engaged to one another.

On 18th September 1907, ACD married Jean Leckie at St Margaret's Church, Westminster, London. The reception was held at The Whitehall Rooms at the Hôtel Métropole and it was attended by both Edalji and Pemberton. During the subsequent honeymoon, ACD received the Order of the Second Class of the Medjideh from Sultan Abdul-Hamid in Constantinople, then the capital of the Ottoman Empire.

In late 1907, ACD and Jean moved into Windlesham. It was here in his study (see Plate 6) that ACD wrote many of his most enduring

Plate 6. ACD at Windlesham.

15

books: *Round the Fire Stories* (1908), *The Lost World* (1912), *The Poison Belt* (1913), *The Valley of Fear* (1915), *His Last Bow* (1917), *The British Campaign in France and Flanders* (1916–1920), *Tales of Adventure and Medical Life* (1922), *Memories and Adventures* (1924), *The Land of Mist* (1926), *The Case-Book of Sherlock Holmes* (1927) and *The Maracot Deep and Other Stories* (1929).

During 1908, ACD was employed by *The Daily Mail* to report upon the Olympic Games, which were being held at White City Stadium in London. During this event, he witnessed the disqualification of an Italian marathon runner called Dorando Pietri for receiving medical attention and a helping hand shortly before crossing the finishing line in first place. Nevertheless, Queen Alexandra presented Dorando with a gold cup in recognition of his efforts and ACD subsequently presented him with a cheque for £308 and a gold cigarette case.

In January 1909, ACD fell seriously ill with an intestinal blockage and underwent an operation at Windlesham. In March of the same year, Jean gave birth to their first son Denis Percy Stewart Conan Doyle. During the summer, ACD assisted a nurse born in Torquay, Miss Joan Paynter, to ascertain the whereabouts of her missing Danish fiancé. He was able to demonstrate to her both where the man had gone and how unworthy this sailor was of her affections!

On the evening of 18th November 1909, ACD gave a lecture entitled *The Congo Atrocity* at Plymouth Guildhall. He was part of a deputation from the Congo Reform Association that sought to publicise the recent ill treatment of the Congolese population by King Leopold II of Belgium. ACD accompanied by a founding member, Edmund Dene Morel – a British journalist, author and socialist politician. The meeting was called at the behest of John Yeo, the then Mayor of Plymouth, who also presided. It was well attended and ACD's lecture was warmly received. Following a vote of thanks proposed by William Littleton (Mayor of Devonport), ACD stated that they would go back with the feeling that the West Country was with them.

Between 7th March and 21st March 1910, ACD and Jean spent a two-week holiday in Cornwall and they resided at Poldhu Hotel, Mullion near Helston. It is interesting to note that, soon after this visit, ACD wrote a Cornwall-based Sherlock Holmes adventure entitled *The Devil's Foot*. This story was first published in *The Strand Magazine* in December 1910.

During April 1910, ACD became interested in the case of Oscar Slater, a German Jew, who was convicted of committing a murder in Scotland (1908). Slater was originally sentenced to hang but this sentence was later commuted to life imprisonment (1909). Thanks partially to the efforts of ACD, Slater was released from prison in 1927 and his sentence was subsequently quashed in 1928.

About 1910, ACD was appointed as the captain of an M.C.C. team that participated in several successive annual cricket tours of Devon. ACD later recalled that during these tours, he played various local teams including Plymouth, Exeter and Devonshire. In October 1910, he was also elected captain of Crowborough Golf Club and president of Crowborough Gymnasium Club. On November 19th of that same year, Jean gave birth to a second son called Adrian Malcolm Conan Doyle.

In 1911, Lady Conan Doyle was made captain of the ladies' section of Crowborough Golf Club. Jean was probably, like most other lady captains, a non-playing member. During the summer, ACD drove a Dietrich-Lorraine car in the Prince Henry's Tour (an Anglo-German motor race that was won by the British). On August 2nd of that same year, ACD's younger brother Innes married a Danish girl called Clara Schwensen in Copenhagen. Towards the end of the year, ACD spoke about finding a fossil footprint near Windlesham. A cast of this footprint can still be seen in the Tunbridge Wells Museum in Kent.

During 1912, ACD introduced a new character called Professor Challenger in a serialisation entitled *The Lost World* that first appeared in *The Strand Magazine* between April and November. A silent film version of this story was the first to be screened on

17

an aeroplane, during a flight, which departed from Croydon Aerodrome on Tuesday 7th April 1925. In August 1912, ACD was placed in charge of the British Olympic Committee ahead of the 1916 Berlin Games that were subsequently cancelled due to the onset of WWI. On 21st December 1912, Jean gave birth to a daughter called Jean Lena Annette Conan Doyle (later Air Commandant Dame Jean Conan Doyle, Lady Bromet).

In March 1913, ACD campaigned for a channel tunnel link between England and France (it was to be another 81 years before one was built). He also organised a gold hunt on Crowborough golf links for six half-sovereigns. The following month, ACD made a speech to the National League for Opposing Woman Suffrage at Tunbridge Wells. Shortly afterwards, acid was poured into a pillar-box outside Windlesham by suffragettes; a policeman was subsequently often stationed at the gate to ACD's home.

During 1914, ACD opened the drill hall of the G2 Crowborough Company of the 5th Battalion Royal Sussex Regiment. He then embarked upon a two-month tour of North America and Canada. Upon his return, WWI began and he formed a volunteer local home guard unit. This body was later replaced by the official 4th Volunteer Battalion of the Royal Sussex, in which ACD served as a private.

In March 1915, the Conan Doyles took a two-week holiday in Torquay, staying at The Grand Hotel. During the afternoon of 27th March, ACD gave an illustrated lecture entitled *The Great Battles of the War* at The Pavilion on the seafront. The meeting was presided over by the local Member of Parliament, Colonel Charles Rosdew Burn. ACD described the events surrounding the commencement of WWI through to the First Battle of Ypres (19th October – 22nd November, 1914). He paid 'high tribute to the Devons' (The Devonshire Regiment) and urged young men to give their strength, '...the rich man his money, the workman his labour, and the women their husbands and sons'.

After the Dublin Easter Rising of 1916, ACD campaigned for the reprieve of Sir Roger Casement, a founder member of the

Congo Reform Association, who was convicted of treason. On this occasion, his intervention failed and Casement was hanged at Pentonville Prison. In the same year, ACD announced his full conversion to Spiritualism in an article entitled *A New Revelation. Spiritualism and Religion* that was published in the psychic magazine, *Light*. ACD later stated that the 'subject of psychical research is one upon which I have thought more and about which I have been slower to form my opinion, than upon any other subject whatsoever.'

On 28th October 1918, ACD's eldest son, 25-year-old Captain Arthur Alleyne Kingsley Conan Doyle, died from post-war pneumonia, having been weakened by wounds received during the Battle of the Somme. Barely four months later, ACD's 45-year-old brother Brigadier-General Innes Hay Doyle, also died from pneumonia.

The Twilight Years

On the afternoon of 4th August 1920, ACD gave a lecture entitled *Death and the Hereafter* at Exeter Hippodrome. This meeting was presided over by F.T. Blake, the then President of the Southern Counties Union of Spiritualists. The following evening he delivered the same lecture at Torquay Town Hall, to an audience composed largely of women. On this occasion the meeting was presided over by one Henry Paul Rabbich, the then President of Paignton Spiritualist Society and Vice-President of the Southern Counties Union of Spiritualists. ACD later recalled that the Town Hall 'was next to a church, and just as I started to speak the church bells began ringing, and I had to shout all the time.' During this visit, ACD stayed with Rabbich at his home called 'The Kraal', situated at 5 Headland Grove, Preston, Paignton. Rabbich was also a prominent local builder and a Freemason at Torbay Lodge No. 1358.

On 11th August 1920, ACD sailed for Australia where he delivered a further series of lectures about Spiritualism. During this tour, ACD learnt that his mother, 83-year-old Mary Doyle, had died on 30th December 1920. Over the course of the following 3 years, ACD continued to lecture on Spiritualism in New Zealand, France, England, Scotland, the United States of America and Canada.

On 20th February 1923, ACD and Jean returned to Devon for the final time. They stayed at the Victoria Hotel, Belgrave Road, Torquay. The following evening, ACD delivered a lecture entitled *The New Revelation* at The Pavilion. This meeting was presided over by G. H. Tredale, the then Mayor of Torquay. On 22nd February, ACD and Jean travelled to Plymouth and stayed at the Grand Hotel. The following evening, ACD delivered the same lecture to an audience at Plymouth Guildhall. This meeting was presided over by one W. H. Watkins on behalf of Solomon Stephens, the then Mayor of Plymouth. It is interesting to note that the Grand Hotel is located next to Elliot Terrace where ACD had lived with George Turnavine Budd in 1882. This might explain why he was prompted to write in detail about this experience in his autobiography, *Memories and Adventures*, that was first serialised in *The Strand Magazine* between October 1923 and July 1924.

During 1924, ACD became interested in the case of the so-called 'chicken run murder'. This crime was committed at Blackness in Crowborough and a certain Norman Thorne was subsequently convicted for it. ACD felt that this judgement was unsafe because it was based largely upon circumstantial evidence. He raised these concerns in letters to the press, but to no avail; Thorne was hanged at Wandsworth Prison on 22nd April 1925.

Between October 1921 and April 1927, *The Strand Magazine* published the last collection of Sherlock Holmes short stories. These stories were collected and republished as *The Case-Book of Sherlock Holmes*, which was published by John Murray in June 1927. It is generally agreed that this final collection of tales is the weakest of all the collections of Holmes stories.

During the winter of 1928, ACD began a tour of several African nations in order to promote Spiritualism. He returned to England during the spring of 1929, having also visited both Egypt and Malta. Just six months later, ACD gave a series of lectures about Spiritualism in the Netherlands, Denmark, Sweden and Norway. He returned home exhausted and suffered a heart attack. ACD rallied a little during the spring of 1930 but then collapsed once again and resigned himself to the prospect of death, which, of course, he perceived as a new beginning and not as an end. Indeed, ACD remarked in a letter: 'I wait with a mind which is full of contentment. I have had many adventures. The greatest and most glorious awaits me now.'

Despite his declining health, on 1st July 1930, ACD led a deputation to the Home Secretary, John Robert Clynes, to promote the cause of Spiritualism. Just six days later, ACD suffered a heart attack in his bedroom next to his first-floor study. At his request, he was moved to a chair by a window that overlooked Crowborough Common and Golf Course. His sons, Denis and Adrian, had raced-off to Tunbridge Wells to fetch oxygen – unobtainable in Crowborough at the time – but it did not help. At 8.17 a.m. on Monday 7th July 1930, ACD died at his beloved home, Windlesham, surrounded by many members of his family.

On 11th July 1930, ACD was buried in his back garden at Windlesham. Very many local and national dignitaries attended the accompanying funeral service. ACD's grave was situated beneath a copper beech tree and close to his writing hut. The original grave marker was made from British oak and it bore an inscription that read 'Blade Straight, Steel True'. Later, this was replaced by a gravestone and inscription that read 'Steel True, Blade Straight'. On 13th July of that same year, a memorial service was also held at the Albert Hall.

Lady Jean Conan Doyle continued to live at Windlesham until her death on 27th June 1940. She was buried in the plot next to ACD. On the sale of the Windlesham estate in 1955, the two bodies were exhumed and re-buried in the graveyard of All Saints Church, Minstead, Hampshire, close to one of ACD's former homes at Stoney Cross in the New Forest (see Plate 7).

Plate 7. The grave of ACD and the second Lady Conan Doyle.

Chapter Two

Dr George Turnavine Budd
(3rd November 1855 – 28th February 1889)

Plate 8. Dr George Turnavine Budd.
COURTESY OF MACDONALD & JANE'S (LONDON).

Introduction

Doctor George Turnavine Budd (hereinafter GTB) was an extremely charismatic personality. During the 1880s, he became a well-known physician in the East Stonehouse area of what is now the city of Plymouth (see Plate 8). Like Bertram Fletcher

23

Robinson, who was also living in Devon at this time, GTB is chiefly remembered for his association with ACD. However, GTB was a formidable character in his own right and had he lived beyond his thirties, there seems little doubt that his name would have become more widely known.

Unfortunately, there has been a tendency to confuse GTB with other members of his family, in particular with two of his uncles, Dr George Budd and Dr John Wreford Budd. In the case of the first uncle, this confusion evidently stems from their shared name and profession. Confusion with the second uncle probably results from the fact that both men practised medicine in the Plymouth area within a decade of one another and each acquired a well-deserved reputation for their eccentric bedside manner. Furthermore, in 1858 a third uncle, Dr Samuel Budd of Exeter, had a son, also named George. This George Budd elected to study medicine during the early 1880s as had his grandfather, father, six uncles and at least two cousins before him, one of whom was GTB.

The association between GTB and ACD began whilst both men were studying medicine at Edinburgh University in 1879. Crucially, GTB was in his final year and some four years older than ACD. He later employed ACD as a junior partner at his surgery in the affluent town of East Stonehouse. During their brief medical partnership, ACD resided with GTB and his young wife in a splendid apartment overlooking Plymouth Hoe. However, ACD was concerned by his partner's unorthodox approach to medicine and soon departed, despite the fact that this placed him in a precarious professional and financial situation.

There is certainly something unusual about ACD's relationship with GTB. ACD was often forthright in his manner towards others and yet he was very circumspect in his treatment of GTB. For example, on 22nd February 1923, ACD revisited Plymouth and stayed at the Grand Hotel, just several yards from where he had once lived with GTB. This trip clearly evoked memories because, in November 1923, ACD had an article entitled *My First Experiences in Practice* published in *The Strand Magazine*. In

October 1924, a slightly revised version of this article was republished as the sixth chapter of his autobiography. In both cases, ACD used the pseudonym 'Dr James Cullingworth' to refer to GTB, despite the fact that his former friend and senior partner had died some 35 years before. It has been suggested that ACD adopted this approach in order to protect the reputation of Budd's descendants. This chapter aims to elaborate upon what is already known about GTB and the nature of his relationship with ACD.

'Budding' Partners

GTB was born on 3rd November 1855 at 28 Park Street, Clifton, Bristol (now Blackwell's Bookshop at 89 Park Street). He was one of nine children born to a successful and eminent physician, Dr William Budd, and his wife, Caroline (née Hilton). Both GTB and his elder brother, Arthur James Budd (14th October 1853 – 27th August 1899), received their early education at Clifton College. On 4th October 1872, Arthur was admitted to Pembroke College, Cambridge, to read for the Tripos degree (B.A.). Shortly afterwards, William Budd developed a chronic cerebral disease from which he never fully recovered. In 1877, Arthur gained his degree and briefly relocated to Edinburgh where GTB was already studying medicine.

Throughout his medical studies (1875–1880), GTB periodically played rugby for a Scottish club called Edinburgh Wanderers (see Plate 9). During the 1877–78 season, Arthur Budd also represented Edinburgh Wanderers and was elected captain. Around March 1878, both brothers relocated to London. GTB became a medical assistant and rented rooms from one Henry Henly at 11 Craven Street, The Strand, Westminster. Arthur enrolled himself as a medical student at the nearby St Bartholomew's Hospital Medical College. Both brothers then played rugby for Blackheath throughout the 1878–79 season (see Plate 10).

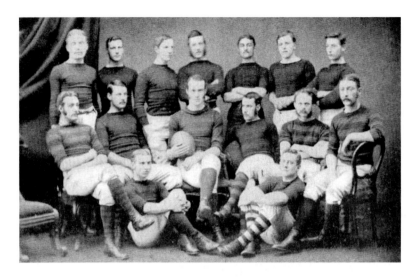

Plate 9. The 1876–77 Edinburgh Wanderers Rugby Football Club
(George Turnavine Budd is standing second from the right).
THE PATRICK CASEY COLLECTION.

During 1879, GTB fell in love with a 17-year-old ward of chancel called Kate Russell. She was a resident of an orphanage run by one Charles Chapman at 12 Percy Villas, Norwood, London. Kate had been born in 1862, at Windsor in Berkshire, and her late father was an army officer called Major Gustavius Russell.

On 21st September 1879, GTB married the underage Kate at a registry office in The Strand; this ceremony was conducted by one John Jeffrey (Superintendent Registrar) and was attended by two independent witnesses called Anthony Holt and Charles Greene. GTB falsely declared that he was a 'Civil Engineer' and Kate falsely declared that she was 18 years old. It is interesting to note that GTB's uncle, Dr George Budd, had previously married one Louisa Matilda Russell (15th August 1854) and they then resided in London for ten years. Perhaps Kate Russell was therefore already related to the Budd family through this previous marriage.

In October 1879, GTB returned to Edinburgh with his young

26

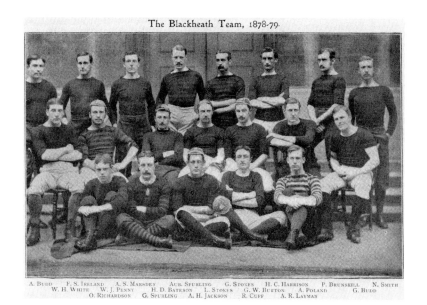

The Blackheath Team, 1878-79.

A. Budd   F. S. Ireland   A. S. Marsden   Aub. Spurling   G. Stokes   H. C. Harrison   P. Brunskill   N. Smith
W. H. White   W. J. Penny   H. D. Bateson   L. Stokes   G. W. Burton   A. Poland   G. Budd
O. Richardson   G. Spurling   A. H. Jackson   R. Cuff   A. R. Layman

Plate 10. The 1878–79 Blackheath Rugby Football Club that included both
George Turnavine Budd and Arthur James Budd.
THE PATRICK CASEY COLLECTION.

wife and was befriended by ACD. ACD later wrote that the Budd's
elopement had caused a 'scandal'. He also reported that the newly-
weds had selected a honeymoon destination by searching *Bradshaw's
Railway Companion* for a place neither of them had visited before.
GTB reputedly tried to disguise himself by dyeing his hair black, but
the dye took unevenly and produced a startling striped effect that did
not wash out for years. The newly-weds then rented 'four small
rooms over a grocer's shop' in Edinburgh and ACD was compelled
to sit on piles of medical books during visits to their sparsely
furnished home.

During the 1879–80 rugby season, GTB emulated Arthur Budd
by being elected captain of Edinburgh Wanderers Rugby Football
Club. Over the course of that season, Edinburgh Wanderers played
eight matches, winning three and losing five. Evidently, ACD

27

sometimes attended these games because he observed that GTB was 'somewhat handicapped by the fury with which he played'. Meanwhile, Arthur had already played rugby for England on three occasions and was to play a further two times. Interestingly, Arthur's final international took place on 19th March 1881 (see Plate 11), just some 13 months or so before GTB entered into medical partnership with the Scottish born ACD. Later, ACD made the following comment about the rugby prowess of the Budd brothers in his autobiography although he does not refer to either of them directly by name:

> He [GTB] was up to international form, and his younger brother [sic] was reckoned by good judges to be about the best forward who ever donned the rose-embroidered jersey of England.

Plate 11. The England Rugby Team that played Scotland on 19th March 1881. Arthur Budd, wearing his 'rose-embroidered jersey' stands third from left.
THE PATRICK CASEY COLLECTION.

28

It is worth noting that ACD confused the respective ages of the Budd brothers in this description. This is perhaps understandable given the 44 years after he first met GTB. Arthur Budd served as a joint vice president of the Rugby Football Union between 1886 and 1888 and was appointed president for the 1888–1889 season. On 30th September 1889, he chaired a meeting that led to the foundation of the London Society of Rugby Football Referees and was also elected its first ever secretary. In 1897, he co-authored a book entitled *Football* with Bertram Fletcher Robinson and others for the *Suffolk Sporting Series* (see Chapter 3). This collaboration was probably prompted by another Blackheath player, Percy Holden Illingworth, who was Fletcher Robinson's flatmate and later the best man at his wedding.

On 9th January 1880, 68-year-old William Budd died from complications relating to the cerebral disease that had afflicted him since 1873. Not long after, his widow, Caroline May Budd, left the West Country to reside with her eldest son, Arthur, at 32 Charlesville Road, Fulham. Arthur was then employed as a solicitor, indicating that he had previously withdrawn from his medical studies.

During August 1880, GTB was awarded both a first class Bachelor's degree in Medicine and a Masters degree in Surgery from Edinburgh University. He then decided to relocate to Bristol in order to take over his father's once thriving practice. Unfortunately, William's lingering illness had necessitated frequent convalescent trips to France, Switzerland and the rural English counties. Perhaps for this reason, GTB found that the practice had sunk too low for it to be revived and before long he was deep in debt. Ironically, in 1965 a 'William Budd Health Centre' was opened at Knowle West in Bristol and it is now one of the largest practices in the area.

Around March 1881, GTB sent a telegram to ACD imploring him to provide both help and advice. At that time, ACD was working as a medical assistant to Dr Reginald Hoare in Birmingham. Nevertheless, ACD travelled to the West Country and advised GTB to meet with his creditors, explain his difficulties and then offer to repay them after making a fresh start elsewhere. This GTB did, and either the creditors believed him, or his wealthy family rallied to his aid because by the 3rd April 1881, he was residing at East Stonehouse in Devon.

The Medical Partnership

In June 1881, GTB opened a surgery at his home at 1 Durnford Street in East Stonehouse. During the following winter, Kate gave birth to their first child, a daughter called Margaret. About the same time, GTB leased an adjacent coach house and stables at 10 Barrack Place. The site of GTB's former surgery was until recently marked with a commemorative plaque that was stolen in 2003 (see Plate 12).

This plaque erroneously overstated the duration of ACD's connection with the surgery and the significance that this stay in Devon had upon his later work, *The Hound of the Baskervilles*. However, it is interesting to note that, in this story, Sherlock Holmes refers to a newspaper called the *Western Morning News*. ACD almost certainly read a regional newspaper *The Western Morning News* during his seven-week partnership with GTB in East Stonehouse during 1882.

The move to Durnford Street seems to have marked an upturn in GTB's fortunes because records reveal that on 16th November 1881 he also acquired a third lease for a property known as Higher Luxmore at Higher Leigham (near Eggbuckland, on the outskirts of Plymouth). GTB agreed to pay an annual rent of £50 over a three-year period for this property that comprised a large house, a stable, a coach house and more than three acres of meadowland. The tenancy was due to commence on 25th December 1881, but it is not known whether he ever actually resided at this address. In any event, during the spring of 1882, GTB sent ACD the following telegram:

Plate 12. The plaque that once marked the site of 1 Durnford Street.

> Started here last June. Colossal success. Come down by next train if possible. Plenty of room for you. Splendid opening.

Clearly, GTB was desirous of an immediate response to this message because he quickly sent a second and more demanding telegram that read:

> I have seen thirty thousand patients in the last year. My actual takings have been over four thousand pounds. All patients come to me. Would not cross the street to see Queen Victoria. You can have all the visiting, all surgery, all midwifery. Make what you like of it. Will guarantee three hundred pounds the first year.

ACD was reluctant to give up his job in Birmingham, but he felt

31

compelled to give this proposition a try. ACD travelled to Plymouth by train during the late spring of 1882 and was greeted by an exuberant GTB in an impressive carriage at the station. This reception must have been remarkably different from the one ACD had received upon his arrival in Bristol just some 14 months or so earlier.

From Plymouth Railway Station, ACD was driven to the Budd residence at 6 Elliot Terrace on Plymouth Hoe. Clearly, between 16th November 1881 and the late spring of 1882, GTB had leased this fourth property and relocated there with his family. ACD was duly impressed by this imposing six-storey Victorian mansion. However, upon closer inspection he discovered that the plush furnishings were confined to the first-floor landing and that the rest of the house was unfurnished. GTB led ACD to believe that the entire property was his and that he would eventually refurbish it. Records now reveal that GTB merely co-leased this property with the nearby Royal Western Yacht Club and Grand Hotel. When ACD was shown to his bedroom he found it contained only a bed and a packing case, upon which stood a hand basin. GTB hammered some nails into the wall so that ACD might hang up his clothes.

ACD recalls in his autobiography that a strange incident occurred one evening after dinner. GTB encouraged him to hold up a small object and thereupon shot a dart at it with an airgun. GTB triumphantly exclaimed that he had hit plumb centre, but ACD denied this and held up his finger with the dart sticking out of it as proof. GTB was so apologetic that ACD felt compelled to laugh-off this incident. Upon examining what he had taken to be a coin, ACD found it to be a medal that was inscribed thus:

Presented to George Budd for Gallantry in Saving Life, January 1879.

ACD questioned GTB about this and was informed that his senior partner had been presented with the medal for rescuing a drowning boy. ACD was prepared to be impressed but GTB dismissed the matter lightly. GTB told him that anyone could pull a child out of the water; the tricky part was getting him to enter it in the first place. GTB also added:

> Then there are the witnesses; four shillings a day I had to pay them, and a quart of beer in the evenings. You see you can't just pick up a child and carry it to the edge of a pier and throw it in. You'd have all sorts of complications from the parents.

Later, young Kate Budd asked ACD not to take too much notice of her husband's bravado. She maintained that the medal had indeed been awarded to GTB for rescuing a boy from the ice, at great risk to his own life.

On another occasion, GTB suggested to ACD that they should publish a newspaper called *Scorpion* and then use it to 'sting' the Mayor and Corporation of Plymouth. GTB planned to write a political commentary and proposed that ACD might contribute a serialised novel. The Mayor of Plymouth at this time was one John Shelley but it is not clear why GTB might wish to publicly criticise him and other local officials.

ACD was also struck by the situation that greeted him at 1 Durnford Street and 10 Barrack Place. Both of these properties were filled to overflowing with waiting patients. Many of these were probably ex-patients of GTB's uncle, Dr John Wreford Budd, who had run a popular practice at nearby 5 Princess Square until his death in 1873. The influence wielded by the Budd family in medical circles at this time cannot be underestimated. One young doctor, having failed several times to start his own practice in Devon, remarked that one had to become a 'Buddist' in order to prosper in the county. GTB's grandfather and several of his other uncles had also worked as physicians in Exeter and North Tawton (located seven miles north-east of Okehampton).

ACD observed that GTB lost no time in abusing his patients roundly. On one occasion, he reportedly refused to treat an obese patient because he ate and drank too much. GTB advised this man to knock down a policeman, go to prison and return upon his release in the unlikely event that treatment was still required! On another occasion, when consulted by a woman complaining of a 'sinking feeling', he suggested she try drinking a glass of wine each day and then swallowing the cork because '...there's nothing better than cork when you are sinking'! ACD reflected that the scene was as good as any pantomime.

ACD was also amazed by the sign on the surgery door advertising free consultations. He asked GTB how he made any money and was told that whilst the consultations were free the medicines were not. Evidently, GTB lavishly prescribed drugs that were generally prepared and dispensed on-site by Kate Budd.

GTB provided ACD with a consultation room and promised him all home visits and surgery. However, after three weeks in practice, ACD had earned just 53 shillings (£2 13s.) and became doubtful as to whether he could make a living. GTB suggested ACD was unduly timid and that people expected their doctor to bully them. However, this approach to patient care was not to ACD's taste.

The Split and Its Aftermath

GTB presumably still had obligations towards his creditors in Bristol. Furthermore, he had recently acquired a new junior partner in the shape of ACD and held four leases on the properties in Durnford Street, Barrack Place, Higher Leigham and Elliot Terrace. The stress of these ever-spiralling financial commitments must have taken its toll on the mental health of GTB because, in a state of paranoia and self-denial, he accused ACD of ruining his business. ACD felt that this was grossly unfair and offered to leave, but GTB fell ill and so he remained to run the surgery.

GTB appeared to be grateful and offered to help ACD start up his own medical practice elsewhere. However, unbeknown to ACD, the Budds had regularly intercepted letters sent to him by his mother, Mary Doyle. She, perhaps intuitively, or advisedly, had expressed the opinion that GTB was a bankrupt swindler and a blackguard. GTB did not read ACD's defensive replies and wrongly concluded that he shared his mother's sentiments. He then hatched a plot to turn the tables upon ACD by offering to post him £1 per week and thereafter, discontinuing this support so that ACD could no longer meet his debts and would be bankrupted. During June 1882, an unsuspecting ACD decided to start his own surgery and he 'went prospecting to Tavistock in Devon but could not see anything to suit'. He then decided to board a steamer bound for Portsmouth and appears to have arived there around 24th June.

By 1st July 1882, ACD had opened a surgery at 2 Bush Villas in Southsea, Hampshire. GTB wrote to ACD accusing him of writing hurtful comments to his mother. He claimed to have read scraps of a torn-up letter found by Kate Budd in ACD's room. Coincidentally, ACD had the very same letter to which GTB referred in his pocket whilst he read his former partner's missive. GTB then discontinued all financial assistance to ACD. Ironically, though ACD did find it hard to make a good living as a doctor in both Southsea and, latterly, London, these financial difficulties were not prompted by the devious intents of GTB. In a sense, it was lucky that the young ACD experienced hardship because he increasingly turned to writing in order to supplement his income.

Following this split, GTB's finances went from bad to worse. On 29th September 1882, he surrendered the lease on Higher Luxmore and was forced to pay £38 in compensation to his landlord, a farmer called Benjamin Butland of Leigham Barton, Eggbuckland. By 1885, GTB had also relinquished the lease on his rooms at 6 Elliot Terrace and was compelled to return with his growing family to 1 Durnford Street. This must have been a source of acute embarrassment to a man who had once made a point of walking home through the professional district of Plymouth clutching his day's takings in full view of other physicians. This dramatic reversal in fortunes undoubtedly stemmed from accumulating debts, exasperated by a dwindling practice. The reduction in patient numbers was probably a result of his practice of combining free consultations with the lavish prescription of drugs. GTB was reportedly criticised by the local coroner on more than one occasion for his lack of regard to the side effects of these drugs, although no case was ever brought against him.

GTB did not fare well with his personal affairs either. During the eight years or so that he and Kate lived together in the Plymouth area they had five children. These were, in order of their birth: Margaret (final quarter of 1881), Iolanthe (first quarter of 1884), Kate (28th November 1885), Mildred (7th June 1887) and William (30th April 1888). Kate died just one hour after her birth from 'congestion of the lungs' and William (named after GTB's father) died aged five days because of 'debility from birth'. GTB certified both the birth and death of his only son and was undoubtedly distressed when he died. William Budd was buried at Ford Park Cemetery, Mutley, Plymouth on 6th May 1888. Reportedly around this same time, GTB became convinced that someone was trying to poison him. Consequently, he would often sit down to his meals surrounded by complicated apparatus designed to test his food before he ate it.

In January 1889, eight months after the death of William, 33-year-old GTB wrote his Last Will and Testament. This document was witnessed by a local solicitor, John G. Hellard, and his clerk, John Howard. Both these men were employed by the firm of Bewes, Hellard & Bewes in East Stonehouse. On 11th February 1889, Kate Budd paid £6 to Ford Park Cemetery in Plymouth for the freehold of the plot, in which her son was buried. GTB died on 28th February 1889. The preceding events suggest that he was invalided and unable to work prior to his death.

GTB's death was certified by Dr Henry Green (of 117 Edith Road, West Kensington, London) who had graduated from

Queen's College in Birmingham in 1856 and was a Licentiate of the Society of Apothecaries. The precise nature of the relationship between GTB and Dr Green is unknown. The official cause of death is recorded as 'Morbus Cerebri' (disease of the brain). It is notable that GTB's father (William) and brother (Arthur) also died from brain diseases, aged 68 and 45 respectively. In 1995, Dr David Nigel Pearce, a physician from Torquay, suggested that the cause of GTB's dementia was either a brain tumour (meningioma) or, more probably, neurosyphilis (a sexually transmitted infection). The latter condition might partially explain his striking appearance, violent mood swings and bouts of paranoia and depression.

GTB was buried in the same grave as his recently deceased son. Recent conservation work undertaken by cemetery staff in conjunction with the authors has revealed that this grave contains a collapsed monumental surround. The edging of this surround comprises sand, cement, slate and ceramic tiles that are similar to those used in the manufacture of Victorian fireplaces. Cemetery staff concluded that this monument was probably homemade, further supporting the view that GTB was suffering from a chronic ailment that precluded him from making an income prior to his death.

GTB's death was announced in both *The Western Morning News* (2nd March 1889) and *The Times* (4th March 1889). On 16th March, a short obituary was published in *The British Medical Journal*. It recalled that GTB had contributed three papers to the journal: *On Amyloid Degeneration*, *The Nature of Rheumatic Symptoms* and *Position of White Corpuscles*. The same article reports that GTB had made other contributions to *The Lancet* and that he was survived by a widow and four children. However, other records reveal that only three children outlived their father.

GTB had stipulated that a friend called William Chilcott should act as one of two joint executors to his Will. Chilcott was a 'Chief Fleet Engineer' at Her Majesty's Dockyard in Devonport.

Perhaps he had assisted GTB in formulating some of his many novel ideas for inventions, all subsequently rejected by the local Admiralty Board. These plans included supplying body armour to prone soldiers and magnetic devices for deflecting cannonballs from naval ships. The other joint executor was GTB's barrister uncle from Bristol, Francis Nonus Budd. However, Francis renounced this responsibility for reasons that perhaps related to his nephew's scandalous marriage.

GTB's estate was subsequently proved at £565.5s.0d gross and £186.18s.1d net. The large discrepancy between these two sums suggests that considerable payments had to be made to creditors and that GTB did indeed die in straitened circumstances. Kate Budd inherited the balance of the estate.

After GTB's death, Kate and her three daughters, Margaret, Iolanthe and Mildred, remained at 1 Durnford Street with a certain Dr William E. Corbett. *The Plymouth, Devonport and Stonehouse Street Directory* indicates that Dr Corbett practised medicine at this address until about 1899. Corbett was twice elected Chairman of the East Stonehouse Urban District Council (1902–1904 and 1913–1914) and he oversaw the amalgamation of East Stonehouse with Plymouth on 1st November 1914. The same records reveal that Kate and her daughters left Durnford Street between 1892 and 1893. It is not known where they went initially. However, the 1901 English Census lists a 39-year-old Berkshire born widow called Kate Budd residing at 1 Douglas Road, Lewisham. She is recorded as 'living on her own means' with two Plymouth born daughters named Margaret and Mildred aged 19 and 13 years respectively. The fate of 15-year-old Iolanthe Budd is unknown.

Challenging Legacy?

GTB appears to have made a profound impression upon ACD because he is featured in two of his books, thinly disguised as 'Dr

James Cullingworth'. The first of these is *The Stark Munro Letters*, published by Longmans, Green and Co. Ltd. in 1895. The second is ACD's autobiography, *Memories and Adventures*, referred to earlier. In this work Cullingworth is described as follows:

> In person he was about 5ft 9in in height, perfectly built, with a bulldog jaw, bloodshot deep-set eyes, overhanging brows, and yellowish hair as stiff as wire, which spurted up above his brows. He was a man born for trouble and adventure...

In 1912, ACD published *The Lost World* that features the larger-than-life character of Professor George Edward Challenger (see Plate 13). It is widely held that Challenger was based upon Professor William Rutherford who had taught both GTB and ACD at Edinburgh University. The novel's hero, Edward Malone, describes his first encounter with Challenger thus:

> His appearance made me gasp. I was prepared for something strange, but not for so overpowering a personality as this. It was his size, which took one's breath away – his size and his imposing presence. His head was enormous, the largest I have ever seen upon a human being. I am sure that his top-hat, had I ventured to don it, would have slipped over me entirely and rested on my shoulders. He had the face and beard which I associate with an Assyrian bull; the former florid, the latter so black as almost to have a suspicion of blue, spade-shaped and rippling down over his chest. The hair was peculiar, plastered down in front in a long, curving wisp over his massive forehead. The eyes were blue-grey under great black tufts, very clear, very critical, and very masterful. A huge spread of shoulders and a chest like a barrel were the other parts of him which appeared above the table, save for two enormous hands covered with long black hair.

Plate 13. The Lost World by Arthur Conan Doyle.
(Henry Frowde, Hodder and Stoughton, London 1914)

Despite the evident physical differences between Professor
Challenger and 'Dr Cullingworth' the two characters share some
personality traits. For example, Challenger has '...a bellowing,
roaring, rumbling voice...' and is very forthright in his dealings
with others. Similarly, Cullingworth is inclined to bully his patients
by shouting abuse at them. Both Cullingworth and Challenger
might also be viewed as scientific egotists who are apt to devise
innovative and ingenious contraptions. It is, therefore, possible that
ACD based Challenger partly on GTB as well as Rutherford.

ACD published three Professor Challenger novels: *The Lost
World* (1912), *The Poison Belt* (1913) and *The Land of Mist*

(1925). All three stories were originally serialised in *The Strand Magazine* between April and November 1912, March and July 1913, and July 1925 to March 1926 respectively. These tales were followed by two further short stories, *When the World Screamed* and *The Disintegration Machine*, which also made their first appearance in *The Strand Magazine* from April to May 1928, and January 1929 respectively. These last two stories were republished in July 1929 in *The Maracot Deep and Other Stories*.

At least seven films have been made featuring the character of Professor Challenger, and one television series. The first of these was *The Lost World*, produced in 1925, with Wallace Beery as Professor Challenger. The last full-length film, called *King of the Lost World*, was made in 2005 and starred Bruce Boxleitner as Challenger. Perhaps the legacy of GTB persists through some of the traits displayed by the Professor as well as through this character's Christian name.

Chapter Three

Bertram Fletcher Robinson
(22nd August 1870 – 21st January 1907)

Plate 14. The 1893–94 Cambridge University Rugby Football Team that
included Bertram Fletcher Robinson (seated second from right).
COURTESY OF THE PATRICK CASEY COLLECTION.

Introduction

Bertram Fletcher Robinson (hereinafter BFR) was a remarkable
character. He is perhaps best remembered for assisting ACD with
the general plot and local details for the most famous of all his
books, *The Hound of the Baskervilles* (1902). But why should

43

ACD, a successful 42-year-old writer, have chosen BFR, a seemingly unknown 30-year-old journalist, to assist him with what transpired to be his most famous literary legacy?

BFR had in fact achieved a great deal by the time his friendship with ACD began aboard the steamship *Briton* in July 1900. Between 1882 and 1890 he attended Newton Abbot Proprietary College in Devon where he was awarded subject prizes for Scripture, English and History (this school was incorporated into Kelly College at Tavistock in 1940). Whilst at 'Newton College' BFR also edited his school magazine that was entitled *The Newtonian* (1887–1889). Between 1890 and 1894, he studied at Cambridge University and won 'Colours' for representing Jesus College in both rugby and rowing. BFR also became a triple rugby 'Blue' (see Plate 14) and would have played for England but for an 'accident'. During 1893, he was appointed sub-editor of an undergraduate magazine called *The Granta* and was awarded a History degree. The following year, BFR narrowly missed being selected for the annual Oxford and Cambridge Boat Race and he was also awarded a Law degree. On June 17th 1896, BFR accepted an invitation to the Bar at the Inner Temple thereby qualifying as a barrister-at-law. During 1897, he began writing regularly for *Cassell's Family Magazine* (later renamed *Cassell's Magazine*) and was also awarded a Master of Arts degree from his Alma Mater.

In early 1900, BFR was employed by Cyril Arthur Pearson to work as a journalist in South Africa for the *Daily Express* newspaper. On 4th April 1900, he dispatched his first by-lined report, *Capetown for Empire* (published 4th May 1900). Between 18th February 1893 and 30th June 1900, BFR wrote nineteen poems, one lyric, one playlet, twenty-five extended articles, one short story and thirteen by-lined reports. He also wrote one book, co-wrote three books and edited seven books about sports and pastimes for *The Isthmian Library*.

Shortly after his return to England on 28th July 1900, BFR was promoted to debut editor of the *Daily Express*. During 1904, he began writing a series of eight short stories that were later featured as chapters in a book entitled *The Chronicles of Addington Peace*. This book is listed in *Queen's Quorum*, as one of the 106 (later 125) most significant short detective/crime stories ever published. By 1905, BFR had been appointed editor of an influential weekly periodical called *Vanity Fair*. During early 1906, he was short-listed as a prospective Liberal Party parliamentary candidate for the constituency of Mid-Devon. In November 1906, BFR was appointed editor of an illustrated weekly periodical entitled *The World – A Journal for Men and Women* that was managed by Max Pemberton and owned by Lord Northcliffe (Alfred Harmsworth).

On Monday 21st January 1907, BFR died from complications relating to typhoid (peritonitis), which he had contracted during the previous month whilst visiting the Paris Automobile Show. He was buried at St Andrew's Church in Ipplepen on Thursday 24th January 1907 and a simultaneous memorial service was held for him at St Clement Danes Church, The Strand, London. Amongst the many people who mourned BFR's death were ten friends, each of whom received a knighthood during their lifetime.

During the six-and-a-half years between his departure from Cape Town and his death, BFR either wrote or co-wrote three books, five poems, three lyrics, eight playlets (four with P.G. Wodehouse), nineteen extended articles, fifty-four short stories and one hundred and fifteen by-lined reports. He also edited one further book for *The Isthmian Library* and contributed one item to a 1906 anthology of twelve short stories entitled *Great Short Stories: Volume 1 Detective Stories* (ACD also contributed two stories to this same book). Furthermore, BFR made contributions to the plots of three other stories, two Sherlock Holmes tales written by ACD (see below) and one story entitled *Wheels of Anarchy* that was written by Max Pemberton (1908).

The Hound of the Baskervilles

On 11th July 1900, both BFR and ACD departed Cape Town

Plate 15. The SS *Briton.*
COURTESY OF THE TOPFOTO COLLECTION

for England aboard a ship called SS *Briton* (see Plate 15). The pair shared a dining table and were photographed together shortly before it docked at Southampton on 28th July (see Plate 16). ACD wrote in his autobiography that it was during this voyage that he 'cemented' his friendship with BFR. This statement implies that the two men had met previously, probably at the Reform Club in London, to which both belonged. ACD also recalled that during the voyage, a French Army officer called Major Roger Raoul Duval accused the British of using dum-dum bullets during the Second Boer War campaign. ACD reacted angrily to this allegation and BFR helped to reconcile the dispute. BFR's friend, Harold Gaye Michelmore (see Plate 17), a Devon based solicitor, coroner and fellow 'Old Newtonian', later reported in a letter published in *The Western Morning News* that during this voyage:

> ...Fletcher Robinson told Doyle the plot of the story which he intended writing about Dartmoor, and Conan Doyle was so intrigued by it that he asked Fletcher Robinson if he would object to their writing it together.
>
> It may be interesting to recall that during the same voyage Fletcher Robinson asked Conan Doyle if it had occurred to him how easy it would be to implicate a man

Plate 16. BFR (seated centre) and ACD (behind his left shoulder) aboard the
SS *Briton* during July 1900.

47

Plate 17. Harold Gaye Michelmore (circa 1950).
COURTESY OF HAROLD MICHELMORE SOLICITORS.

in a murder crime if you could obtain a finger-print of his in wax for reproduction in blood on a wall or some other obvious place near the seat of the crime.

Conan Doyle was taken by the idea and asked Fletcher

Robinson whether he intended to use it in his own literary work. Fletcher Robinson replied: 'not immediately,' and Conan Doyle offered him 50 pounds for the idea which Fletcher Robinson accepted, and Conan Doyle incorporated the idea in one of the Sherlock Holmes tales which he published shortly afterwards.

Thus it appears that BFR and ACD agreed to co-author a Dartmoor-based story during their voyage aboard the SS *Briton*. However, it is unlikely that 'the story' bore much resemblance to *The Hound of the Baskervilles*. Perhaps 'the story' to which Michelmore referred was one of two other Dartmoor-linked stories that BFR had published after the various versions of *The Hound of the Baskervilles* were printed (1901/02). The first of these was a fairy-tale entitled *The Battle of Fingle's Bridge*, which was published during May 1903 in *Pearson's Magazine* (Vol. 15, pp. 530–536). The second was a short story entitled *The Mystery of Thomas Hearne* which featured as the fifth chapter of a 1905 book written by BFR called *The Chronicles of Addington Peace* (London: Harper & Brother). ACD subsequently used BFR's finger-print idea in a Sherlock Holmes short story entitled *The Adventure of the Norwood Builder* that was first published in *Collier's Weekly Magazine* (1903).

On Thursday 25th April 1901, BFR visited the home of a friend and author called Max Pemberton (see Plate 18). He had previously edited BFR's first book entitled *Rugby Football* and subsequently commissioned him to write various pieces for *Cassell's Family Magazine* and *Cassell's Magazine*. During dinner, Pemberton related a story to BFR that resonates to some extent with the legend featured in *The Hound of the Baskervilles*. Sir Max Pemberton later reported the following relevant details in an interview that was published in the London *Evening News*:

The late Fletcher Robinson, who collaborated with Doyle in the story, was dining at my house in Hampstead one night

Plate 18. Max Pemberton (circa 1905).
COURTESY OF THE TOPFOTO COLLECTION.

when the talk turned upon phantom dogs. I told my friend
of a certain Jimmy Farman, a Norfolk marshman, who
swore that there was a phantom dog on the marshes near St
Olives [now called St Olaves near Great Yarmouth,
Norfolk] and that his bitch had met the brute more than

50

once and had been terrified by it. 'A Great black dog it were,' Jimmy said, 'and the eyes of 'un was like railway lamps. He crossed my path down there by the far dyke and the old bitch a'most went mad wi' fear...Now surely that bitch saw a' summat I didn't see...'

Fletcher Robinson assured me that dozens of people on the outskirts of Dartmoor had seen a phantom hound and that to doubt its existence would be a local heresy. In both instances, the brute was a huge retriever, coal black and with eyes which shone like fire.

Fletcher Robinson was always a little psychic and he had a warm regard for this apparition; indeed, he expressed some surprise that no romancer had yet written about it. Three nights afterwards, Fletcher Robinson was dining with Sir [sic] Arthur. The talk at my house was still fresh in his mind and he told Doyle what I had said, emphasising that this particular marshman was as sure of the existence of the phantom hound as he was of his own being. Finally, Fletcher Robinson said 'Let us write the story together.' And to his great content Sir [sic] Arthur cordially assented.

The dinner to which Pemberton refers took place on Sunday 28th April 1901 at the Royal Links Hotel in Cromer, Norfolk. ACD was still recovering from a recent recurrence of typhoid and clearly intended to spend a therapeutic golfing weekend with BFR (Friday 26th – Monday 29th April). However, it is unlikely that the pair actually played much golf because local weather records reveal that this weekend was generally overcast, damp, cold and breezy (the mean daily temperature and wind-speed were 7°C and 20.7mph). Nevertheless, an entry in ACD's accounts book reveals that he paid £6 to the 'Royal Links Hotel' by Tuesday 30th April. Furthermore, on Saturday 4th May 1901, the weekly *Cromer & North Walsham Post* reported that ACD had recently taken 'a short stay at the Golf Links Hotel'. Thereafter, a journalist called J.E. Hodder Williams, writing for the British version of a periodical called *The Bookman*, reported that during this trip to Cromer, BFR had:

> ...mentioned in conversation some old-country legend which set Doyle's imagination on fire. The two men began building up a chain of events, and in a very few hours the plot for a sensational story was conceived and it was agreed that Doyle should write it.

The legend that reputedly fired ACD's imagination appears to have been that of Black Shuck, which Pemberton had related to BFR over dinner some three days before. Black Shuck was reportedly a large, solitary hound with glowing eyes that roamed the Norfolk coastline. In some tales, Black Shuck would ascend from the beach at Cromer to nearby Cromer Hall on a path that was adjacent to the Royal Links Hotel. Whilst at Cromer, ACD wrote a letter to his mother in which he stated as a footnote:

> Fletcher Robinson came here with me and we are going to do a small book together 'The Hound of the Baskervilles' – a real creeper.

ACD also wrote a second letter to Herbert Greenhough Smith, the editor of *The Strand Magazine*, in which he again described the story as a 'real creeper'. ACD offered the story to Greenhough Smith but insisted that, 'I must do it with my friend Robinson and his name must appear with mine.' He added, 'I shall want my usual 50 pounds per thousand words for all rights if you do business.'

During early May 1901, ACD decided that the book would need some masterful central figure and reflected, 'Why should I invent such a character when I have him already in the form of Sherlock Holmes?' He again contacted Greenhough Smith and offered him a second version of the same novel, a version that would incorporate Holmes. Greenhough Smith agreed to pay ACD £100 per thousand words for the Holmes version.

Research Trips to Dartmoor

Much has been written over the years about the nature of the literary collaboration between ACD and BFR that ultimately led to the inception of *The Hound of the Baskervilles*. It is generally accepted that ACD and BFR spent about one week together exploring the Dartmoor area during the early summer of 1901. However, there has been a good deal of uncertainty and disagreement surrounding the precise details of this visit. For example, it is not known whether ACD and BFR travelled to Devon together, where they stayed, the impact of this visit upon the narrative of the story, or the precise dates for the visit itself. However, new information now makes it possible to reinterpret what was previously known and deduce the following account of the visit.

It appears that shortly before Saturday 25th May 1901, BFR made a preliminary research trip to Dartmoor with a friend called The Revd Robert Duins Cooke (see Plate 19). The weather throughout the preceding 24 days of this month on Dartmoor was generally 'very fine' (the mean daily temperature, wind speed and rainfall were 9°C, 10.5mph and 0.00433in respectively). The Revd Cooke was the vicar of St Andrew's Church in Ipplepen where BFR's father, Joseph Fletcher Robinson (see Plate 20), had been acting as churchwarden for 19 years. In a letter published in *The Western Morning News*, The Revd Henry Cooke reported the following:

> Sir – May I add to Mr. H. G. Michelmore's interesting letter on 'The Hound of the Baskervilles.' My father – Prebendary R. D. Cooke – was Vicar of Ipplepen at the date you mention, 1901. He was a great authority on Dartmoor. Mr. B. F. Robinson asked his advice and help in planning the background of his story.
>
> My father and Mr. Robinson went up to the Moor together, and under my father's guidance the details of the

Plate 19. The Revd R.D. Cooke and family (1926).
COURTESY OF WENDY MAJOR.

background were filled in on the spot! My father was very proud of this and often told his children how he had helped to write a very well known book.

My sister, Mrs. Graeme, of Shaldon, has a copy of the book presented to my father by Mr. B. F. Robinson, and inscribed: 'To Rev. R. D. Cooke from the assistant plot producer, Bertram Fletcher Robinson.'

At or about the same time that BFR visited Dartmoor with The Revd Cooke, ACD was playing in a two-day cricket match at Lords in London. This match finished on Friday 24th May ahead of a busy Bank Holiday weekend. On Sunday 26th and Monday 27th the train service from London to Devon was substantially reduced. Therefore, it appears likely that a solitary ACD made the five to six hour journey from Paddington to Newton Abbot on the morning of Saturday 25th. He then arrived at Newton Abbot

Plate 20. Joseph F. Robinson.
COURTESY OF MEADE-KING, ROBINSON & CO. LTD.

Railway Station no earlier than late that same afternoon. ACD was collected by a coachman called Henry 'Harry' Baskerville (see Plate 21). Harry was employed by Joseph Fletcher Robinson and shared the same Christian name and surname as a central character within *The Hound of the Baskervilles*. Despite claims to the contrary by ACD's son, Adrian Conan Doyle, it seems likely that ACD was then driven 3.5 miles (or 40 minutes) to the Robinson family home at Ipplepen. Conversely, it is unlikely that

Plate 21. Henry 'Harry' Baskerville at work for the Sawdye family (1912).
COURTESY OF WENDY MAJOR.

Plate 22. Arthur H. Marshall (1920).
COURTESY OF THE TOPFOTO COLLECTION.

ACD consented to being driven for 22 miles (or four hours) to Princetown directly.

The weather on Sunday 26th May was showery (0.14in), persistently overcast and cold (11°C). It therefore seems unlikely that ACD and BFR would have elected to visit Dartmoor on this day. Instead, they appear to have accompanied BFR's parents to the morning service at St Andrew's Church in Ipplepen (led by The Revd R.D. Cooke). Later, it was recalled by witnesses that ACD's visit to the church 'was looked upon with disapproval by some of the parishioners, who knew him at that time to be a leading spiritualist'. In fact at that time, ACD was agnostic and merely interested in psychical research.

Between Monday 27th and Wednesday 29th May, the weather improved substantially (the mean daily temperature was 15°C and there was zero rainfall). Consequently, Harry drove BFR and ACD to nearby locations including Heatree House, Bovey Tracy and Hound Tor (collectively these three locations are closer to Park Hill House than Princetown). On Thursday 30th May, they were prevented from visiting Dartmoor by a 'severe storm' during which time 1.3in of rain fell at Ashburton and 1.95in of rain fell at Princetown. Harry later reported that whilst at Park Hill House, ACD and BFR would occupy the billiards room and that 'sometimes they stayed long into the night, writing and talking together'.

On Friday 31st May 1901, it appears that Harry drove BFR and ACD from Park Hill House (altitude 249ft) to Princetown (altitude 1368ft). The shortest route between these two locations in 1901 was 20 miles along narrow and undulating lanes (average ascent of 55ft per mile). This journey would have required approximately four hours to complete and thereby precluded a return journey to Park Hill House on the same day. For this reason, BFR and ACD decided to prolong their visit to this area and resided at the Duchy Hotel in Princetown until Sunday 2nd June.

Between Friday 31st May and Sunday 2nd June, the weather at

Princetown was persistently overcast, cold (average 10°C), showery (total 0.23in) and moderately breezy (average 15mph). Later, a Californian born journalist and writer called Henry James Wells Dam published an article entitled *Arthur Conan Doyle – An Appreciation of the Author of 'Sir Nigel', the Great Romance Which Begins Next Sunday*, in the *Sunday Magazine* supplement of the *New York Tribune*. This article features BFR's recollections about his trip to the high moorland area about Princetown with ACD in the summer of 1901:

> One of the most interesting weeks that I have ever spent was with Doyle on Dartmoor. He made the journey in my company shortly after I told him, and he had accepted from me, a plot which eventuated in the 'Hound of the Baskervilles'. Dartmoor, the great wilderness of bog and rock that cuts Devonshire at this point, appealed to his imagination. He listened eagerly to my stories of ghost hounds, of the headless riders and of the devils that lurk in the hollows – legends upon which I have been reared, for my home lay on the borders of the moor. How well he turned to account his impressions will be remembered by all readers of 'The Hound'.
>
> Two incidents come especially to my recollection. In the centre of the moor lies the famous convict prison of Princetown. In the great granite buildings, swept by the rains and clouded in the mists, are lodged over a thousand criminals, convicted on the more serious offences. A tiny village clusters at the foot of the slope on which they stand, and a comfortable old-fashioned inn affords accommodation to travellers.
>
> The morning after our arrival Doyle and I were sitting in the smoking-room when a cherry-cheeked maid opened the door and announced 'Visitors to see you, gentlemen'. In marched four men, who solemnly sat down and began to talk about the weather, the fishing in the moor streams and

other general subjects. Who they might be I had not the slightest idea. As they left I followed them into the hall of the inn. On the table were their four cards. The governor of the prison, the deputy governor, the chaplain and the doctor had come, as a pencil note explained, 'to call on Mr. Sherlock Holmes'.

One morning I took Doyle to see the mighty bog, a thousand acres of quaking slime, at any part of which a horse and rider might disappear, which figured so prominently in 'The Hound'. He was amused at the story I told him of the moor man who on one occasion saw a hat near the edge of the morass and poked at it with a long pole he carried. 'You leave my hat alone!' came a voice from beneath it. 'Whoi'! Be there a man under 'at?' cried the startled rustic. 'Yes, you fool, and a horse under the man.'

From the bog we tramped eastward to the stone fort of Grimspound, which the savages of the Stone Age in Britain, the aborigines who were earlier settlers than Saxons or Danes or Norsemen, raised with enormous labour to act as a haven of refuge from marauding tribes to the South. The good preservation in which the Grimspound fort still remains is marvellous. The twenty-feet slabs of granite – how they were ever hauled to their places is a mystery to historian and engineer – still encircle the stone huts where the tribe lived. Into one of these Doyle and I walked, and sitting down on the stone which probably served the three-thousand-year-old chief as a bed we talked of the races of the past. It was one of the loneliest spots in Great Britain. No road came within a long distance of the place. Strange legends of lights and figures are told concerning it. Add thereto that it was a gloomy day overcast with heavy cloud.

Suddenly we heard a boot strike against a stone without and rose together. It was only a lonely tourist on a walking excursion, but at sight of our heads suddenly emerging from the hut he let out a yell and bolted. Our subsequent disappearance was due to the fact that we both sat down and rocked with laughter, and as he did not return I have small doubt Mr. Doyle and I added yet another proof of the supernatural to tellers of ghost stories concerning Dartmoor.

It is worth noting that these experiences evidently impressed ACD because he subsequently incorporated an escaped convict from Dartmoor Prison, a bog and an ancient stone hut into the plot of *The Hound of the Baskervilles*. Furthermore, ACD also recorded his reaction to the high moorland in the following letter that he wrote to his mother on Saturday 1st June 1901 from the Duchy Hotel:

Dearest of Mams

Here I am in the highest town in England. Robinson and I are exploring the moor together over our Sherlock Holmes book. I think it will work splendidly – indeed I have already done nearly half of it. Holmes is at his very best, and it is a highly dramatic idea which I owe to Robinson.

We did 14 miles over the Moor today and we are now pleasantly weary. It is a great place, very sad & wild, dotted with the dwellings of prehistoric man, strange monoliths and huts and graves. In those old days there was evidently a population of very many thousands here & now you may walk all day and never see one human being. Everywhere there are gutted tin mines. Tomorrow [Sunday 2nd June] we drive 16 miles to Ipplepen where R's parents live. Then on Monday Sherborne for the cricket, 2 days at Bath, 2 days at Cheltenham. Home on Monday 10th. That is my programme.

Other sources confirm that ACD did, indeed, play in these cricket matches. ACD must have departed for Sherborne on Monday 3rd

June having slept the previous night at Park Hill House. He could not have travelled to Sherborne on Sunday 2nd June because the only two trains to this destination departed from St David's Station in Exeter at 01.38 and 15.09 (the Penzance to Waterloo service). ACD was unable to catch the first train because he was still in Princetown at that time. Furthermore, he was unable to catch the second train because the only available interconnecting train between Newton Abbot Station and St David's Station left the former station at 09.25. This left insufficient time for a 'weary' ACD to travel from Princetown via Park Hill House to Newton Abbot Railway Station. It is far more probable that the following day, a rested ACD caught the 07.55 train from Newton Abbot Station to St David's Station (arriving at 08.45) and then the 09.02 hours train from St David's Station via Yeovil Junction to Sherborne (arriving at 11.14). ACD was then probably driven the mile (or ten minutes) between Sherborne Station to Sherborne School.

The Hound Narrative

By mid-May 1901, ACD had sent the proof for the first instalment of *The Hound of the Baskervilles* (Chapters I–II of XV) to the offices of *The Strand Magazine*. Records belonging to Sidney Paget, the artist employed to illustrate *The Hound of the Baskervilles*, reveal that he was paid £34 13s. at the end of May for completing seven illustrations to accompany this first instalment. On Saturday 25th May 1901 (the same day that ACD appears to have met BFR in Devon), the following announcement appeared in *Tit-Bits* that like *The Strand Magazine*, was also published by George Newnes:

> Very many readers of The Strand Magazine have asked us over and over again if we could not induce Mr. Conan Doyle to give us some more stories of this wonderful

character. Mr. Conan Doyle has been engaged on other work, but presently he will give us an important story to appear in the Strand, in which the great Sherlock Holmes is the principle character. It will appear in both the British and American editions. In America the play founded upon the career of the great detective has run for many months with enormous success. It is going to be produced in London in about three months, and at the same time the new Sherlock Holmes story will commence in the Strand. It will be published as a serial of from 30,000 to 50,000 words, and the plot is one of the most interesting and striking that have [sic] ever been put before us. We are sure that all those readers of the Strand who have written to us on the matter, and those who have not, will be very glad that Mr. Conan Doyle is going to give us some more about our old favourite.

On Monday 17th June 1901, the proof for the second instalment of *The Hound of the Baskervilles* (Chapters III–IV of XV) was returned to ACD at his home in Surrey. He then informed the editor of *The Strand Magazine* that the third instalment (Chapters V–VI of XV) was almost complete. Given that ACD was absent from his home between Thursday 16th May (playing cricket in London) and Monday 10th June, it seems probable that the second instalment and much of the third instalment was written at Park Hill House between Saturday 25th and Friday 31st May. This theory would explain why ACD stated in the letter that he wrote to his mother on Saturday 1st June that he had 'already done nearly half of it'. Furthermore, it might also partially explain why BFR's author friend, Arthur Hammond Marshall (see Plate 22), wrote the following comments in his autobiography:

He [BFR] loved a story, and was a great inventor of them. He gave Conan Doyle the idea and plot of The Hound of the Baskervilles, and wrote most of its first instalment for the Strand Magazine. Conan Doyle wanted it to appear under their joint names, but his name alone was wanted, because it was worth so much more. They were paid £100 per thousand words, in the proportion of three to one. As I put it to Bobbles [BFR] at the time, "Then if you write 'How do you do?' Doyle gets six shillings and you get two." He said that he had never been good at vulgar fractions, but it sounded right, and anyhow what he wrote was worth it.

The extent to which BFR contributed to the narrative of *The Hound of the Baskervilles* remains a contentious issue. Nevertheless, Marshall's assertion that BFR 'wrote most of its first instalment' is undoubtedly incorrect. Perhaps Marshall simply mistook the ideas that BFR evidently contributed to Chapters I–III and subsequent payments made to him by ACD as evidence that he contributed directly to this part of the narrative? Nevertheless, it is true that BFR made important contributions to the first two instalments. For example there are references to hunting-to-hounds and local legends within the account of the Baskerville Legend that is communicated to Sherlock Holmes by Mortimer in Chapter II. Furthermore, in Chapter III, Holmes outlines various fictional Dartmoor settings to Dr Watson that are frequently based upon actual locations. BFR wrote about these subjects and it is fair to say that his knowledge in respect to such matters was superior to that of ACD.

At the end of June 1901, ACD sent the fourth and fifth instalments (Chapters VII–IX of XV) to *The Strand Magazine*. During mid-July 1901, ACD went on holiday to the Esplanade Hotel in Southsea, having recently submitted the sixth and seventh instalments of *The Hound of the Baskervilles* (Chapters X–XII of XV). Indeed, ACD sent corrections to *The Strand Magazine* from Southsea. During August 1901, the first of nine monthly instalments of *The Hound of the Baskervilles* appeared in the British version of *The Strand Magazine* (see Plate 23). BFR's contribution was acknowledged in a brief footnote to Chapter I as follows:

> This story owes its inception to my friend, Mr. Fletcher Robinson, who has helped me both in the general plot and in the local details. — A.C.D.

In September 1901, the first of nine monthly instalments of *The Hound of the Baskervilles* appeared in the American version of *The Strand Magazine*. During this same month, ACD was resident at his home called Undershaw in Hindhead and completed writing the final two instalments (Chapters XIII–XV of XV). The story

Plate 23. Cover of the British edition of *The Strand Magazine* (November 1901).

now numbered about 60,000 words meaning that ACD was due to be paid some £6,000 for his serialised narrative.

On 25th March 1902, *The Hound of the Baskervilles* was published as a novel by George Newnes of London (see Plate 24). It preceded by one month the publication of the final episode in the British version of *The Strand Magazine*. This first British book edition includes the following short acknowledgement:

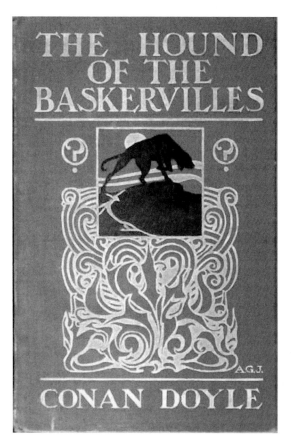

Plate 24. The first British book edition (published 25th March 1902).

MY DEAR ROBINSON,

It was to your account of a West-Country legend that this tale owes its inception. For this and for your help in the details all thanks.

Yours most truly,

A. CONAN DOYLE.

Sometime thereafter, BFR gave first edition copies of *The Hound of the Baskervilles* to The Revd Robert Duins Cooke, Marion Cooke (wife of The Revd Cooke) and Harry Baskerville. BFR wrote an inscription within each of the three books and two of these concede to the limited extent of his involvement with the actualisation of this story:

To Rev. R D Cooke from the assistant plot producer, Bertram Fletcher Robinson

To Mrs. Cooke, with the kind regards of the assistant plot producer, Bertram Fletcher Robinson

To Harry Baskerville from B Fletcher Robinson with apologies for using the name!

On 15th April 1902, *The Hound of the Baskervilles* was published as a novel by McClure, Phillips and Company (New York). This, the first American edition of the book, includes a version of ACD's acknowledgement letter to BFR. This version was written, from dictation, on 26th of January 1902, by Major Charles Terry (ACD's Secretary) and is now held by the Berg Collection in New York Public Library. This version of the acknowledgement therefore predates that which was printed in the first British book edition:

MY DEAR ROBINSON

It was your account of a west country legend which first suggested the idea of this little tale to my mind.

For this, and for the help which you gave me in its evolution, all thanks. Yours most truly, A. Conan Doyle.

Gossip Hounds

In October 1901, shortly after publication of the first instalment of *The Hound of the Baskervilles* within the American version of *The Strand Magazine*, the following remarks appeared in the American version of a magazine entitled *The Bookman*:

Every one who read the opening chapters of the resuscitation of Sherlock Holmes in the September number of the Strand Magazine must have come to the conclusion that Dr Doyle's share in the collaboration was a very small one. The Hound of the Baskervilles opens very dramatically, and promised to be a good tale. But the Sherlock Holmes to whom we are introduced is a totally different personage from the Sherlock Holmes of The Study in Scarlet [sic], The Sign of Four, The Adventures and The Memoirs. Of course all the little superficial tricks and mannerisms have been worked in, but there it ends. In a brief note Dr Doyle, whose name alone is at the head of the story, acknowledges the collaboration of Mr. Fletcher Robinson. Of course the matter is one which concerns primarily only the two authors and their publishers: but we have very little hesitation in expressing our conviction that the story is almost entirely Mr. Robinson's and that Dr Doyle's only important contribution to the partnership is the permission to use the character of Sherlock Holmes.

The American version of *The Bookman* was renowned for publishing literary gossip. This article was probably written by one of its two editors called Arthur Bartlett Maurice because he later by-lined a second article that featured in the same periodical and returned to the topic of authorship. This second item was published shortly after the release of the first American book edition of *The Hound of the Baskervilles* (15th April 1902). In this later article, Maurice echoed the earlier comments, albeit in a slightly more circumspect manner:

> When the subject of this story was first discussed in literary and publishing circles in London there prevailed the idea that Mr. Fletcher Robinson had in hand a story to which Dr Doyle was lending some assistance, his name, and the character Sherlock Holmes. A little later it was being said that Dr Doyle and Mr. Robinson were in collaboration on this new Sherlock Holmes story. Finally, the first instalment of the tale itself appeared as being the work of Dr Doyle alone. Allusion to Mr. Fletcher Robinson was made only in a foot-note, in which the reputed writer courteously, but rather vaguely, thanked Mr. Robinson for one or two hints and suggestions that had been of some value to him in the writing of the story. Just what the meaning of all this was, just how much Mr. Robinson did contribute to the inception and the working out of *The Hound of the Baskervilles*, the reviewer is neither inclined nor prepared to say.

In June 1902, the American version of *The Bookman* published a story entitled *The Bound of the Astorbilts* by a writer called Charlton Andrews. This early parody of *The Hound of the Baskervilles* concluded with the following paragraph:

> As I gazed, from far out upon the moor there came the deep, unearthly baying of a gigantic hound. Weirdly it rose and fell in blood-curdling intensity until the inarticulate

sound gradually shaped itself into this perfectly distinguishable wail: 'I wonder how much of it Robinson wrote?'

This series of allegations and remarks was wholly unwarranted. BFR and ACD remained close friends after the publication of *The Hound of the Baskervilles* and regularly associated prior to BFR's untimely death aged just 36 years on 21st January 1907. For example, in early 1904, ACD, BFR and Pemberton were all elected to an exclusive 12-man criminological society referred to by its members as 'Our Society'. Indeed, just two days after one of the regular meetings of 'Our Society' held at Pemberton's house on 18th October 1906, BFR and ACD are recorded as having played golf at Hindhead in Surrey. Furthermore between 1904 and 1907, BFR wrote several articles in which he praised ACD for his integrity. The last of these articles entitled *People Much Talked About in London* was published posthumously in May 1907 in an American periodical called *Munsey's Magazine* (Vol 37, No 2, pp. 142–143) and reads:

In Pall Mall, too, it is likely that we shall meet some of the more famous of English literary men bound for that most exclusive of clubs — the Athenaeum. Here comes that kindly giant, Sir Arthur Conan Doyle, the creator of Sherlock Holmes, prince of detectives. He is of a fine British type, a clear-headed, sport-loving, big-hearted patriot.

A mention of the Athenaeum Club reminds me of a story Sir Arthur told me of his first visit, after election [8th March 1901], to that home of the respectabilities. He walked up to the hall-porter and, desiring to introduce himself to that important person's notice, asked if there were any letters for Conan Doyle. Now the Athenaeum is a favorite resort of the clerical dignitaries, and the hall-porter, who had small acquaintance with literature, replied 'No, canon, there are no letters for you.'

Sir Arthur did not care to explain, and for some weeks he

suffered much from the disapproving eye of the hall-porter. The suit of tweeds affected by the great novelist shocked that functionary deeply, and when one day Sir Arthur appeared in a long racing-coat, the spectacle had such an effect upon him that Doyle had to rush to the desk and explain that he was not a dignitary of the church, but a writer of tales to whom some latitude in dress might be allowed.

Sir Arthur is an earnest supporter of the rifle-club movement. He has erected targets for a miniature rifle-range at his house on the moors at Hindhead [founded in late 1900]. There you may observe groom and carpenter, mason and village blacksmith competing against one another on a Saturday afternoon in the same fashion as their forebears did with 'The Long' bow, winning Creçy and Agincourt thereby. Among them the novelist may be seen at his best, shooting with them, cheering them on with kindly words or awarding prizes, chiefly out of his own pocket.

Consequently, any suggestion that BFR was less than perfectly content with the outcome of his literary collaboration with ACD must be dismissed. Indeed there is much evidence to support the view that BFR profited directly from his association with ACD. For example, several of BFR's own short stories were accompanied by statements that promoted his involvement with *The Hound of the Baskervilles*. Clearly, ACD was content to let BFR promote his own literary creations through such references. This too signals the respect and friendship that persisted between the two writers.

Due Acknowledgement

The evidence suggests that ACD and BFR had fully intended to write a Dartmoor-based story together whilst aboard the SS *Briton* in July 1900. The theme for this story was settled upon during a subsequent visit to Cromer in late April 1901. Shortly thereafter, ACD introduced the character of Sherlock Holmes and also wrote the first instalment for *The Hound of the Baskervilles*. During late May and early June 1901, BFR and ACD conducted research for the story together in Devon. Clearly, by this stage, the two men had agreed that ACD alone should write the narrative. However, why was BFR seemingly content to withdraw from a full collaboration and instead act as a mere 'assistant plot producer'?

The answer to this question may never be unequivocally resolved. However, it is conceivable that BFR felt that Sherlock Holmes was the intellectual property of ACD and therefore decided to limit his involvement upon the introduction of this character to the story. Alternatively, there are indications that BFR was unable to co-author the narrative for a number of professional reasons. For example, he had some 14 items published in the *Daily Express* and *Pearson's Magazine* during the 16-week period when ACD was writing the narrative for *The Hound of the Baskervilles* (May 1901 – September 1901). Furthermore, he was commissioned to write 25,000 words of 'descriptive letterpress' for a book entitled *Sporting Pictures* that was subsequently published by Cassell & Company Limited in 1902 (edited by E.W. Savory).

BFR also had a number of personal reasons for not contributing directly to the narrative of *The Hound of the Baskervilles*. For example, during 1901, BFR was living with his aged uncle Sir John Robinson (see Plate 25) who was also friendly with ACD. Sir John died on 30th November 1903 and the following year his autobiography entitled *Fifty Years on Fleet Street* was published by McMillan & Company Limited. It includes the following statement made in a foreword written by Frederick Moy Thomas, a friend and employee of Sir John's for 25 years:

I am much indebted to Sir Arthur Conan Doyle for leave to publish his striking letter to Sir John Robinson on the

Plate 25. Sir John Robinson.
COURTESY OF THE TOPFOTO COLLECTION.

subject of America and the Americans; …and to a number
of Sir John's relatives and friends for similar facilities or for
valuable counsel or assistance.

This comment is important for several reasons. Clearly the
Robinson family were still on friendly terms with ACD some
three years after publication of *The Hound of the Baskervilles*. This
further discredits the claims that were made about an authorship
controversy in the American version of *The Bookman*. It also
implies that BFR was unable to contribute directly to the narrative of *The Hound of the Baskervilles* because he was already busy
assisting Sir John with his autobiography. Certainly, BFR had
acquired about seven years of editorial experience through his

involvement with *The Newtonian, The Granta,* the *Daily Express* and *The Isthmian Library*.

Additionally, BFR commenced a courtship with Gladys Morris during 1901 that ultimately led to their marriage on 3rd June 1902. Throughout this period BFR's prospective father-in-law, a retired artist called Philip Morris, was struggling to keep his young family whilst battling a chronic illness that ultimately contributed to his death (22nd April 1902). It seems highly probable that BFR would have paid regular visits to their nearby home at 92 Clifton Hill, St Marylebone, London, in order to assist Philip, Gladys and her two younger siblings in whatever way he could. Similarly, BFR must have been mindful of his own father's growing infirmity and undoubtedly made frequent trips to Ipplepen prior to Joseph's death on 11th August 1903.

So it appears that for the aforementioned professional and personal reasons, BFR was content to assist ACD with the plot of *The Hound of the Baskervilles* but not its narrative. Indeed, ACD confirmed as much in June 1929 when he wrote the following statement in a preface to a collection of four Sherlock Holmes novellas entitled *The Complete Sherlock Holmes Long Stories* (London: John Murray):

> Then came The Hound of the Baskervilles. It arose from a remark by that fine fellow, whose premature death was a loss to the world, Fletcher Robinson, that there was a spectral dog near his home on Dartmoor. That remark was the inception of the book, but I should add that the plot and every word of the actual narrative are my own.

Nevertheless, BFR is deserving of some gratitude for the role he played in inspiring ACD to resurrect Sherlock Holmes who had been 'killed off' in 1894. ACD subsequently wrote thirty-three short stories and one novel featuring Sherlock Holmes, but none ever surpassed the popular success of *The Hound of the Basker-villes*. Since the publication of the first book edition in 1902, there have been no fewer than nineteen related films made in six different languages and many more television adaptations.

In 1912, ACD wrote the book *The Lost World* that featured a character called Edward Malone. It is interesting to note that there are parallels between this character and that of BFR. For example, both spent part of their 'boyhood' in the West Country, fished and exceeded six feet in height. Furthermore they each became accomplished rugby players, London-based journalists and loved a woman called Gladys. Perhaps the character of Malone is therefore ACD's most enduring tribute to his former 'assistant plot producer', BFR.

Chapter Four

The Arthur Conan Doyle Devon Tour

*1) 6 Elliot Terrace, The Hoe, Plymouth

Locate Plymouth Barbican. Continue along Madeira Road, which runs parallel to the walls of the Royal Citadel and Seafront. At the first mini-roundabout, take the second exit for Hoe Road and park in any available pay-and-display bay located on the right. Cross the road and enter The Promenade by way of the disabled car park. Walk 350 yards due west along The Promenade between Smeaton's Lighthouse Tower and the various War Memorials. Elliot Terrace and the Grand Hotel are both located on the right (see Plate 26).

Plate 26. 6 Elliot Terrace (right), Grand Hotel (centre) prior to WWII.

Elliot Terrace is a row of seven imposing six-storey Victorian mansions, constructed around 1873 by Messrs Call & Pethick (John Pethick was Lord Mayor of Plymouth between 1898 and 1900). The name derives from one Colonel James Elliot who once owned most of the land upon which Plymouth Hoe now stands. ACD resided with GTB and his family at number 6 Elliot Terrace following his arrival in Plymouth around early May 1882. ACD later recalled that the property was largely unfurnished and that he was provided with nails upon which to hang his clothes. GTB was content to allow ACD to think that he was the sole tenant of the property, presumably in order to impress him. However, records now reveal that GTB co-leased this property with the Royal Western Yacht Club and the Grand Hotel. Clearly neither the Yacht Club nor Grand Hotel was using 6 Elliot Terrace whilst ACD resided there. It therefore seems probable that the old Grand Hotel vacated Elliot Terrace around 1880 in order to occupy an adjacent building that was newly constructed by John Pethick. ACD resided at the new Grand Hotel on 22nd February 1923.

Visitors might be interested to learn that 3 Elliot Terrace was bought by Waldorf Astor in 1908 (2nd Viscount Astor from 18th October 1919). On 1st December 1919 his wife, Lady Astor, became the first woman Member of Parliament (she represented the Unionist Party) to take up a seat in the House of Commons. She is reported to have told Winston Churchill: 'If you were my husband, I'd put arsenic in your coffee', to which he retorted 'Madam, if I were your husband, I'd drink it!' Lady Astor died on 2nd May 1964 and bequeathed 3 Elliot Terrace to the City of Plymouth. This property is now the official residence of the Lord Mayor of Plymouth and is also used to accommodate visiting dignitaries and circuit judges.

2) Durnford Street, East Stonehouse, Plymouth (1.4 miles)

From Hoe Road, double back to the mini-roundabout off

Madeira Road and then turn right towards Plymouth Dome. Continue for 0.8 of a mile along Hoe Road, Grand Parade, Great Western Road and West Hoe Road. At the roundabout, turn left towards the Continental Ferryport (Millbay Road) and continue for 0.6 of a mile. At the crossroads, keep to the right lane and park for free immediately after this junction outside numbers 12–24 Barrack Place (note that parking is restricted between 10.00 a.m. and 5.00 p.m.).

Durnford Street was constructed in 1773 to provide accommodation for senior naval and military personnel. During June 1881, GTB opened a surgery on the north-eastern side of the crossroads between Durnford Street and Barrack Place (see Plate 27). Around early May 1882, GTB and ACD entered into partnership at this practice but the arrangement was dissolved after only seven weeks. The former surgery and neighbouring buildings were demolished in 1958. The cleared land was later redeveloped and used to site a car dealership called Renwick's

Plate 27. 1 Durnford Street (circa 1920).

Garage. Most recently, the site of the former surgery has been incorporated into a luxury apartment block called Evolution Cove.

Until 2003, the former site of 1 Durnford Street was marked by a commemorative plaque (see Plate 12). A series of twenty-two other plaques featuring quotations from Sherlock Holmes stories can still be seen set within the footpath between 85 and 125 Durnford Street. An additional plaque is mounted within the lower step at the entrance to 93 Durnford Street and reads:

SIR ARTHUR CONAN DOYLE
1859 – 1930

IN 1882 CONAN DOYLE PRACTISED MEDICINE AT NO 1 DURNFORD STREET. UNFORTUNATELY THE RELATIONSHIP WITH HIS PRACTICE PARTNER WAS AN UNHAPPY ONE AND ENDED WITH CONAN DOYLE MOVING TO SOUTHSEA. DURING HIS SPARE TIME FROM HIS MEDICAL PROFESSION HE BECAME MORE INVOLVED IN HIS WRITINGS. 'A STUDY OF SCARLET', THE FIRST OF 68 STORIES FEATURING SHERLOCK HOLMES, APPEARED IN 1887. CONAN DOYLES TIME IN DEVON UNDOUBTEDLY INSPIRED HIS LATER LITERARY WORK, 'THE HOUND OF THE BASKERVILLES.' A HOLMES CULT AROSE AND STILL FLOURISHES TODAY.

This inscription contains a number of factual and grammatical errors. For example, 'A Study of Scarlet' should read 'A Study in Scarlet'; furthermore, it is generally accepted that ACD wrote 60 Sherlock Holmes stories and that his time in Durnford Street did not inspire *The Hound of the Baskervilles*. However, Sherlock Holmes does refer in this story to a newspaper called the *Western Morning News*. ACD almost certainly read an almost identically named regional newspaper, *The Western Morning News*, during his residence in East Stonehouse.

3) Plymouth Guildhall, Royal Parade, Plymouth (3.0 miles)

From Barrack Place, follow the one-way system for 0.2 of a mile to a roundabout and then turn right into Edgcumbe Street (signposted A38). Continue along the A374 for 0.6 of a mile to the crossroads between Union Street and The Crescent. Continue for 0.2 of a mile to Derrys Cross Roundabout and then double back towards the crossroads between Union Street and The Crescent. Just before this crossroads, turn left into The Crescent and continue for 0.3 of a mile to the fourth set of traffic lights. At these lights, turn left into Princess Way, then take the first right into Athenaeum Place. Continue for 0.1 of a mile and then turn left by Plymouth Crown and County Courts. A little further you will come to the Guildhall pay-and-display car park. Visitors may enter the Guildhall reception area and request a free tour of this building (see Plate 28).

In 1909, ACD met journalist Edmund Morel, who had co-

Plate 28. A postcard showing Plymouth Guildhall (right) prior to WWII.

founded the Congo Reform Association in 1904. The CRA wanted to publicise recent oppression of the Congolese population by the former Belgian colonists. During October 1909, ACD had a pamphlet published entitled *The Crime of the Congo* (Hutchinson & Co.). In the preface to this work he wrote: 'There are many of us in England who consider the crime which has been wrought in the Congo lands by King Leopold of Belgium and his followers to be the greatest which has ever been known in human annals.' ACD then embarked upon a three month lecture tour with Edmund Morel to promote agitation against Belgian oppression in the Congo. On 18th November 1909, they visited Plymouth Guildhall and ACD delivered a lecture entitled *The Congo Atrocity*. ACD returned there on 23rd February 1923, to deliver a lecture on Spiritualism, *The New Revelation*.

Like Elliot Terrace, the Guildhall was constructed in 1873 by John Pethick and was officially opened on 13th August 1874 by His Royal Highness Prince Edward, The Prince of Wales (whom later became King Edward VII and knighted ACD). It is a fine example of so-called 'early-pointed' architecture. The original building was gutted by fire during the second night of the Plymouth Blitz (20th–21st March 1941). Restoration work began in January 1953 and the layout of the original building was essentially reversed. The site of the stage upon which ACD delivered his lectures is now at the main entrance to the post-war Guildhall building. There is a plaque commemorating Lord and Lady Astor by the old northern entrance to this building.

4) Ford Park Cemetery, Ford Park Road, Plymouth (5.1 miles)

From Plymouth Guildhall, double back to the junction between Athenaeum Place and Princess Way. Turn right and follow the one-way system to Derrys Cross Roundabout. Join this roundabout and take the third exit for Royal Parade. Continue for 0.5 of a mile to

Charles Cross Roundabout (site of a burned-out church). At this roundabout, take the first exit and continue for 0.3 of a mile along Charles Street and Cobourg Street towards Liskeard (A38) and Tavistock (A386). At North Cross Roundabout, take the second exit for Saltash Road and then continue for 0.3 of a mile in the right lane. At the first mini-roundabout, take the third exit for Central Park Avenue. Continue for 0.3 of a mile, then turn left into Ford Park Cemetery via the lodge-gate entrance. Visitors may park for free next to the two Victorian chapels.

GTB and his son, William, are buried together at Ford Park Cemetery (see Plate 29). ACD used GTB as a model for a character called Dr James Cullingworth and possibly a second character called Professor George Edward Challenger (see Chapter 2). To locate GTB's grave, walk 100 yards down the processional drive towards the lodge-gate entrance and turn right after the Garden of Remembrance. Continue along the tarmac path for 50 yards to the stone steps on the right. Just beyond and to the left of these steps is the grave of Lieutenant James Arthur Reynolds (marked by a large anchor). GTB's grave is sited four rows back from this grave (Plot: CLG, 41, 4). Care should be exercised, particularly during wet weather, as the ground underfoot is slippery and can conceal items that might trip an unwary visitor!

Visitors may also wish to visit the joint grave of GTB's uncle, Dr John Wreford Budd, and his son, Robert Sutton Budd (GTB's cousin). To locate this grave from the car park, walk 40 yards down the processional drive towards the lodge-gate entrance. Take the second grass pathway on the right, then turn right again immediately before a large round tomb. The Budd grave is located on the right some four graves back and two graves in (Plot: D, 26, 17). Visitors are encouraged to enquire at the office adjacent to the new chapel and car park about the Ford Park Heritage Trail. There are many other interesting characters buried at this cemetery, among them a former Mayor of Plymouth, John Pethick (1827–1904), who built Elliot Terrace, Plymouth Guild-hall and the new Grand Hotel (Plot: CHA, 16, 2).

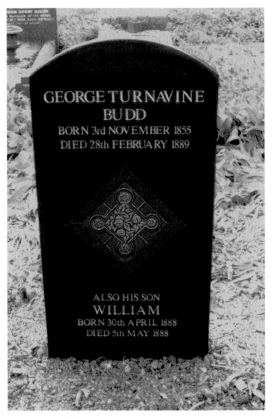

Plate 29. The grave of George Turnavine Budd and his son.

5) The Lopes Arms, Tavistock Road, Roborough (11.5 miles)

From Ford Park Cemetery, double back to the mini-roundabout off Saltash Road. At this roundabout, take the third exit for Alma Road (signposted Saltash, Liskeard and the A38). Continue for 5.4 miles along Alma Road, Outland Road and Tavistock Road (A386) to the third major roundabout by Belliver Industrial

Estate. At this roundabout, take the third exit and double back along Tavistock Road towards Plymouth. After 0.2 of a mile turn left into the old Tavistock Road (signposted Roborough). Continue for 0.2 of a mile past Leatside Walk and Leatside. The Lopes Arms (see Plate 30) is located on the right and visitors may park for free on the road outside these premises. Those wishing to take refreshments at this public house are also permitted to use their car parking facilities without charge.

During June 1882, GTB and ACD dissolved their medical partnership and ACD travelled to Tavistock to investigate the possibility of opening up a his own practice there. During that trip, he visited The Lopes Arms at the boundary between Plymouth and the southern edge of Dartmoor. ACD had a semi-fictional account of a photographic expedition from Plymouth to Tavistock, *Dry Plates on a Wet Moor*, published in the *British Journal of Photography* in November 1882. In this article, ACD

Plate 30. The Lopes Arms, old Tavistock Road, Roborough.

refs to The Lopes Arms as 'The Admiral Vernon Public House'. The same trip undoubtedly inspired the setting for a later Sherlock Holmes story, *The Adventure of Silver Blaze*, first published in the *The Strand Magazine* in 1892.

6) High Moorland Visitor Centre, Tavistock Road, Princetown (21.4 miles)

From The Lopes Arms, continue north along the old Tavistock Road to the junction with the A386. Turn left and return to the roundabout by Belliver Industrial Estate. At this roundabout, take the third exit for Tavistock. Continue for 3.8 miles across Roborough Down to the roundabout at Yelverton. At this roundabout, take the second exit for Princetown and the B3212. Continue for 5.8 miles to the mini-roundabout in Princetown. Here, take the first exit for Tavistock Road (signposted B3357). Continue for 0.1 of a mile, then turn left into Station Cottages Royal Court. Follow signs for the High Moorland Visitor Centre Car Park (a small fee is charged for parking).

The building that now houses the High Moorland Visitor Centre was constructed around 1809 to accommodate officers of the Army and Militia who were guarding Napoleonic prisoners of war at what is now HMP Dartmoor. In 1850, Mr James Rowe acquired this property and reopened it as the Duchy Hotel (see Plate 31). He also installed a beautiful tiled mosaic in the reception area that can still be seen and reads, 'Welcome the coming, speed the parting guest' (from Pope's translation of Homer's Odyssey). On 2nd June 1901, ACD wrote a letter to his mother from the Duchy Hotel (this name is still visible on the north-eastern exterior wall of the building) in which he reported (see Chapter 3):

Here I am in the highest town in England. Robinson and I are exploring the Moor over our Sherlock Holmes book. I think it will work out splendidly – indeed I have already

84

Plate 31. Duchy Hotel (circa 1905).
PHOTOGRAPH BY DAVID GERMAN.

done nearly half of it. Holmes is at his very best, and it is a highly dramatic idea which I owe to Robinson...

In 1990 the Dartmoor National Park Authority began converting the property into the present day Visitor Centre, which was officially opened by His Royal Highness Prince Charles, The Prince of Wales, on 9th June 1993. In the centre shop visitors may view a large photograph of ACD and a mannequin of Sherlock Holmes. The exhibit section includes further information about ACD, BFR and *The Hound of the Baskervilles* (a small donation is requested).

*7) Her Majesty's Prison Dartmoor, Princetown (21.8 miles)

From the High Moorland Visitor Centre, double back to the

mini-roundabout at the entrance to Tavistock Road and take the first exit for Two Bridges (B3212). Continue for 0.3 of a mile to a lay-by on the right, just beyond Princetown. This location provides an excellent view of Dartmoor Prison (see Plate 32).

Originally constructed between 1806 and 1809 to act as a depot for prisoners from the Napoleonic War, the prison was commissioned as a convict gaol in 1850 and has remained so ever since. During the Victorian era, Dartmoor was reputed to have the most severe regime of any British prison and was used to incarcerate the most dangerous convicts. Visitors who wish to learn more about the history of Dartmoor Prison are encouraged to visit its Heritage Centre, located on Tavistock Road in Princetown (free car park with a small fee for entrance to the exhibit area).

Between 31st May and 2nd June 1901, ACD and BFR stayed at the Duchy Hotel. Whilst there, they met the governor, deputy governor, chaplain and physician of Dartmoor Prison (William Russell, Cyril Platt, Lawrence Hudson and William Frew respec-

Plate 32. HMP Dartmoor on a foggy winter's day.

tively). On 13th June 1901, two convicts called William Silvester and Fergus Frith made a well-publicised escape from Dartmoor Prison. At about the same time, ACD was completing the third instalment of *The Hound of the Baskervilles* (Chapters V–VI of XV) and introduced a character called Selden, also a fugitive from Dartmoor Prison.

ACD previously featured Dartmoor Prison in three other stories: *The Sign of Four* (February 1890), *How the King Held the Brigadier* (April 1895) and *How the Brigadier Triumphed in England* (March 1903*).* The first of these stories was the second Sherlock Holmes novel (October 1890) and the others are both Brigadier Gerard stories.

*8) Brook Manor, near Hockmoor Hill, West Buckfastleigh (33.4 miles)

From the lay-by opposite Dartmoor Prison, continue for 1.0 mile to a T-junction, then turn right towards Two Bridges (B3357). Continue for 4.1 miles towards Ashburton before turning right towards Hexworthy, The Forest Inn and Venford Reservoir. Continue for 4.6 miles past Venford Reservoir towards the village of Holne. Upon entering Holne, turn right at the first sign marked Scoriton. Continue for 0.4 of a mile then take the second turning on the right (also signposted Scoriton). Continue past Littlecombe Farm and The Tradesmans Public House for 1.1 miles to a crossroads. Here, turn right towards Buckfastleigh and continue for 0.4 of a mile to a red letterbox mounted in the wall on the left. Visitors can park for free just beyond this letterbox, near the entrance to Hawson Court and Stables. Opposite the letterbox is a five-bar gate from which a good view of Brook Manor (see Plate 33) may be enjoyed.

Brook Manor was constructed in 1656 for Squire Richard Cabell III (1622–1672). An entry in *The House of Commons Journal* for 1647 reported that Cabell was fined by Parliament for

Plate 33. Brook Manor (southern façade).
PHOTOGRAPH BY A. D. HOWLETT © 1992.

siding with the Royalists in the English Civil War. He subsequently retracted his support for Charles I and was pardoned. This act no doubt angered local people who were dependent for their livelihood upon The Duchy of Cornwall Estate. Perhaps for this reason, malicious stories about this unprincipled squire abounded. For example, one night Cabell reputedly accused his wife of adultery and a struggle ensued. She fled to nearby Dartmoor but he recaptured and murdered her with his hunting knife. The victim's pet hound exacted revenge by ripping out Cabell's throat and some say that its anguished howls can still be heard. In reality, Cabell's wife actually outlived him by some 14 years but the legend nevertheless persisted. There are parallels between this story and the legend of the wicked Hugo Baskerville that was reported to Sherlock Holmes by Mortimer in *The Hound of the Baskervilles*. Later Holmes solved the case when he noticed a resemblance between a 1647 portrait of Hugo Baskerville dressed as a Royalist and another character called Stapleton.

9) Holy Trinity Church, Church Hill, Buckfastleigh (35.3 miles)

From Brook Manor, continue for 1.5 miles in the direction of Buckfastleigh to the Round Crossroads. Go straight on for 0.4 of a mile towards the tower of Holy Trinity Church. Visitors can park for free outside the main entrance to this church.

Holy Trinity is primarily a thirteenth-century building but has a fifteenth-century nave. On 8th May 1849, arsonists began a fire that destroyed the vestry and the parish chest. The same fire also badly damaged the communion table and a section of the roof over the northern aisle. During WWII, rogue German bombs shattered some of the stained glass windows. On 21st July 1992, arsonists again attacked the church but on this occasion the ensuing inferno completely gutted the building. Today, Holy Trinity Church is a near empty shell, although services are still held there intermittently during the summer months.

The evidently unpopular Squire Richard Cabell III died in the early summer of 1672 but various versions of the tale about him murdering his wife persisted. Perhaps inevitably, this notoriety has spawned some fanciful local superstitions, and the various misfortunes that have befallen Holy Trinity Church have been linked to the 'sepulchre' or 'penthouse tomb', which the squire had constructed (see Plate 34). It has also been suggested that the heavy tombstone enclosed therein was used to prevent his ghost from escaping to Dartmoor and riding to hounds. However, it is not known for sure whether Squire Richard Cabell III is actually interred within the sepulchre and in any event the tombstone is inscribed only with the names of his father and grandfather who both predeceased him and were also named Richard Cabell. The tombstone has itself been damaged by past acts of vandalism or black magic rites and is now safeguarded by an iron grill.

Plate 34. The sepulchre built by Squire Richard Cabell III (located by the church porch).

10) St Andrew's Church, West Street, Ashburton (38.8 miles)

From Holy Trinity Church, double back to the Round Cross-roads and turn right towards Buckfast. Continue for 0.4 of a mile to the mini-roundabout just beyond the entrance to Buckfast Abbey. Take the second exit and proceed for 0.4 of a mile to another mini-roundabout. Take the first exit for Exeter, Plymouth and Totnes. Cross the bridge that spans the River Dart and then turn left towards Ashburton and Princetown. Continue for 1.7 miles to the T-junction by Pear Tree Service Station; turn left. Continue for 50 yards and then turn right onto Western Road that leads to both Ashburton and Buckland in the Moor (B3352). Continue for 0.5 of a mile, before turning left into Kingsbridge

Lane by the public toilets. Follow signs to the pay-and-display car park. Having parked, leave the car park through an archway located in the south-western corner. Turn right (West Street) and walk 50 yards up the hill to the main entrance for St Andrew's Church, located on the left.

Henry 'Harry' Baskerville is buried in the graveyard here. It will be recalled that he drove ACD and BFR about Dartmoor when the two men researched the setting for *The Hound of the Baskervilles* in 1901 (see Chapter 3). Baskerville also shared the same Christian name and surname as a major character in the book. To locate his grave (see Plate 35) enter the graveyard by way of the main gate and turn right. Walk 100 yards along the tarmac path that runs parallel to a tall stone wall. At the end of this wall, turn right onto a smaller tarmac path by the grave of Richard Bennett. Ascend the hill past 12 rows of graves and turn left at the headstone for Edward Amery Adams. The grave of Henry Baskerville and his wife, Alice (née Perring), is situated 7 plots in from this headstone.

Visitors may be interested to know that two other graves bearing the names of characters featured in *The Hound of the Baskervilles* can be found nearby. To locate the graves of 'James Mortimer' and George 'Perkins', return to that of Richard Bennett. Mortimer's is 3 rows up and 4 plots in while Perkins' is 2 rows up and 12 plots in.

*11) 'Dorncliffe', 18 West Street, Ashburton (38.8 miles)

Return to the main entrance for St Andrew's Church and turn right. Walk 50 yards to Ashburton Methodist Chapel where the funeral service for Henry 'Harry' Baskerville (see Plate 36) was held on 31st March 1962. Situated directly opposite is number 18 West Street or 'Dorncliffe' (see Plate 37), once home to Henry and Alice Baskerville.

Baskerville worked for the Robinson family for some 20 years

Plate 35. The grave of Henry 'Harry' Baskerville and his wife.

until about 1905 when Emily Robinson was admitted to Spring-field Nursing Home in Newton Abbot. He then moved to Ashburton where he worked as a gardener and coachman for 52 years for an influential local family called Sawdye (see Plate 21). Initially, Baskerville resided with his family in East Street (circa 1905–08) and then at 'Laburnums' (circa 1909–31). Thereafter, he resided at 18 West Street until his death in 1962 aged 91 years. Whilst in Ashburton, Baskerville was elected to the Urban District Council where he served for eight years, became a member of the Court Leet and Baron Juries and was also elected

Plate 36. Henry 'Harry' Baskerville (circa 1955).

Chairman of the Co-operative Society, a post he held for twelve years. He was also a member of Ashburton Methodist Church and had held the offices of Circuit Steward, Society Steward, Poor Steward and Trustee. On 6th February 1961, Baskerville was interviewed at 'Dorncliffe' by Douglas Cock for local BBC Radio, when he made the following comments relating to *The Hound of the Baskervilles*:

'...Conan Doyle came and I fetched him from Newton Abbot Station, he remained at Park Hill for eight days and

Plate 37. 'Dorncliffe', 18 West Street, Ashburton.

I took him back again, I also took him around Bovey Tracy and Heatree...to have a look around Hound Tor and...pick up some of the threads of the story. The book was written and they promised me the first issue...which I had...As a young man I didn't think anything about sending my copy...to Conan Doyle to have him [sic], autographed...not till after the film came out and then I thought well what a stupid [sic], I haven't sent the book to Conan Doyle...'

During this short interview, Baskerville is frequently muddled. The film to which he refers was the 1959 Hammer Films production of *The Hound of the Baskervilles* starring Peter Cushing (Holmes), André Morell (Watson) and Christopher Lee (Sir Henry Baskerville). Baskerville had enjoyed wide publicity prior to the release of this film, which has led some to suggest that he overstated his role and that of BFR in the creation of the story.

12) Recreation Ground, Coach Road, Newton Abbot (46.2 miles)

From the car park, follow the one-way system to North Street. Turn right and continue for 0.1 of a mile to a T-junction. Turn left into East Street (B3352) and follow all signs for Exeter, Newton Abbot and the A38. Join the Exeter bound carriageway of the A38 and continue for 0.7 of a mile. Join the A383 (signposted Newton Abbot) and continue for 5.0 miles to the first roundabout in Newton Abbot. Take the second exit, sign posted Town Centre, Totnes and A381. Continue for 0.3 of a mile to the traffic lights by the ASDA superstore and turn right. Continue for a 0.2 of a mile, then turn right onto Wolborough Street (sign posted Totnes and A381). Continue for 0.4 of a mile and turn left into Old Totnes Road. Continue for 0.2 of a mile towards the tower of St Mary the Virgin Church. Continue for 0.5 of a mile along Coach Road to Newton Hall, situated on the left. After Newton Hall, take the first turning on the right, this leads to the headquarters of the Devon County Football Association. Utilise the free parking on the left, adjacent to the Recreation Ground.

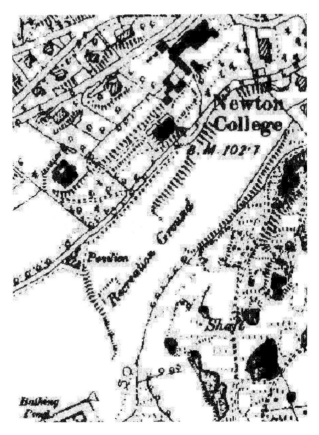

Plate 38. A map showing the layout of Newton College (circa 1890).

Between 1882 and 1890, BFR was a dayboy at Newton Abbot Proprietary College. The campus (see Plate 38) comprised of a recreation ground, a cricket pavilion (see Plate 39), a gymnasium, multiple racquet and fives courts, a bathing pond, a chapel, reading and sitting rooms, a library, a laboratory, classrooms and two sizable boarding houses called School House and Red House. Adjacent to the senior campus was a third junior boarding house called Newton Hall. Other notable Old-Newtonians include the

Plate 39. A postcard featuring the cricket pavilion at Newton College (circa 1900).

author, Sir Arthur Quiller-Couch (1863–1944) and the explorer, Colonel Percy Harrison Fawcett (1867–1925). It is interesting to note that Quiller-Couch met ACD on 6th March 1892. Furthermore, it has been suggested that accounts of Fawcett's expedition to the borderland between Bolivia and Brazil (1906–1909) partly inspired ACD to write *The Lost World* (1912).

'Newton College' shut in 1939 and most of the remaining boys and staff transferred to Newton House at Kelly College in Tavistock (1940). The former 'Newton College' campus was reopened as Forde Park Home Office Approved School (1940–1973). Devon County Council then used the site as a home for vulnerable young people. Most recently the site was sold to Barratt Developments PLC and the buildings demolished and replaced with modern homes. However, the 'Newton College' recreational ground still exists and is used jointly by Devon County Council, Devon County Football Association and Newton Abbot Athletic Football Club. The last organisation incorporated the original

97

pavilion into its new clubhouse. The bathing pool was filled in and is now the site of Decoy BMX track.

*13) Park Hill House, Park Hill Cross, Ipplepen (49.2 miles)

From the former grounds of Newton College, double back to St Mary the Virgin Church. Continue for 0.4 of a mile to a round-about and take the first exit for Totnes (A381). Continue for 2.1 miles to Park Hill Cross Service Station on the left, some 200 yards beyond the entrance to the village of Ipplepen. Visitors wishing to use the facilities offered at this service station can park for free on the forecourt. Park Hill House (see Plate 40) is situated directly opposite Park Hill Cross Service Station. This property is best viewed from atop the grassy bank, beside the footpath, that runs alongside the service station.

Park Hill House was constructed around 1850 for a cider merchant called John Bowden. This estate also included a nearby

Plate 40. Park Hill House.

98

farm, outbuildings and many acres of land. In 1866, John Bowden also funded the construction of Ipplepen Methodist Chapel. By 1878, he was trading as a 'Corn Factor, Commission and General Merchant' in Plymouth and the neighbouring Parish of Wolborough-with-Newton Abbot. By 3rd April 1881, the Bowden family had relocated to 22 Lambourn Road, Clapham, London and Park Hill House was left unoccupied. Meanwhile, Joseph Fletcher Robinson and his second wife, Emily Robinson (née Hobson), were residing at 6 Lyndhurst Road, Wavertree near Liverpool. Ten-year-old BFR was boarding at a small school called Penkett Road Beach House in Liscard, near New Brighton, in West Cheshire.

Shortly after 3rd April 1881, Joseph retired as the commercial manager of Meade-King, Robinson & Company Limited, a firm of merchants that he had founded around 1866 (this company still trades). By Easter 1882, Joseph and his family had relocated to Ipplepen, situated some 270 miles to the south of Liverpool. One possible reason for this move is that Joseph wished to retire to an area that would enable him to pursue his interest in equestrian sports. Indeed, it is feasible that he visited Devon between 1848 and 1866, whilst working as a commercial traveller for Robert Sumner & Company of Liverpool. Furthermore, he may have visited Park Hill House itself, in order to continue trading with John Bowden (a 'Cider Merchant' of that same name is listed in *Gore's Directory for Liverpool* until 1849). Interestingly, a 'Bowden' later witnessed BFR's marriage to Gladys Morris on 3rd June 1902 in London.

Between 25th May and 3rd June 1901, ACD visited Devon to conduct research for *The Hound of the Baskervilles*. It is probable that, between 25th and 30th May, he resided with BFR and his family at Park Hill House. During this period, ACD also appears to have written the second and much of the third instalment of the story (Chapters III–IV and V–VI of XV respectively). ACD and BFR then returned to Park Hill House on 2nd June after visiting Princetown. The coach house used to garage the vehicle

in which ACD and BFR travelled about Dartmoor with Baskerville is now called Park Hill Lodge and is situated two doors to
the left of Park Hill House (beside Moor Road).

*14) 'Honeysuckle Cottage', 2 Wesley Terrace, East Street, Ipplepen (49.7 miles)

From Park Hill Cross Service Station, turn left onto the A381
towards Totnes. Continue for 100 yards, then turn right into
Foredown Road (signposted Ipplepen, Torbryan and B'hempston).
Continue for 0.4 of a mile to a staggered crossroads where East Street
merges with Bridge Street (just beyond the entrance to Ipplepen
Methodist Chapel). At this crossroads, turn right into Dornafield
Road and continue for 50 yards. Visitors can park for free on the left,
just beyond the entrance to Brook Road. Walk 50 yards to the
entrance of the chapel, then a further 20 yards along East Street to
'Honeysuckle Cottage', 2 Wesley Terrace (see Plate 41).

Henry Matthews Baskerville was born in the neighbouring
village of Dainton during February 1871. His father, John Baskerville, was a farm labourer and had married Mary Mathews on
17th March 1854. The Baskervilles already had two children,
John (also a farm labourer) and Mary Catherine, aged eleven and
eight years respectively.

Around 1886, Joseph Fletcher Robinson employed Henry as a
'Domestic' at Park Hill House. Initially, his duties consisted of
pumping water to the house from a nearby well, polishing silver-
ware and cleaning out fireplaces. By 1891, he had assumed the
additional duties of 'Coachman and Groom' and was paid 12
shillings and 6 pence per week. Later, Henry became head
coachman and was responsible for one assistant coachman, three
coaches and two horses. He worked for the Robinson family for
about 20 years until around 1905.

In 1891, Henry was residing with his parents and his uncle and
namesake, Henry Matthews (a retired coachman), at what is now

Plate 41. Wesley Terrace.

2 Wesley Terrace. On 17th November 1894, Henry married Alice Perring at the Wesley Church in Torquay and thereafter resided at number 3 Wesley Terrace (or 'Wisteria Cottage'). Henry and Alice had two daughters called Myrtle Alberta (born autumn 1895) and Eunice Freda (born summer 1902). By 31st March 1901, Baskerville's parents had relocated to nearby 'Credefords'.

15) St Andrew's Church, Ipplepen (50.1 miles)

From Dornafield Road, double back to the staggered crossroads beside the chapel and turn right into Bridge Street. Continue for 0.4 of a mile towards Ipplepen Village Hall, then bear right into Silver Street. After 50 yards, park for free on the left, opposite the sign for Orley Road. Cross the road and enter St Andrew's Church through the main gate.

To locate BFR's grave from the main gate (see Plate 42) turn left before the first grave that belongs to the parents of Henry Baskerville. Continue for 50 yards past the north-western corner of the church and towards the Church Hall. Turn left just beyond the grave of Arthur William Poole and just before the iron gate at the entrance to the Church Hall. Continue for another 20 yards towards the first and largest monument bearing a cross. BFR is buried next to his parents and just 20 yards to the north of The

Plate 42. BFR's grave in the north-western section of St Andrew's Church.

Revd Robert Duins Cooke, who assisted him in mapping out the provisional fictional setting for *The Hound of the Baskervilles*.

Visitors are encouraged to visit the chancel inside the church where they will locate two stained-glass windows that are dedicated to the Robinson family. The Victorian artist C.E. Kemp, who also produced windows for Westminster Abbey in London, designed both of these windows. The southern window was commissioned by Emily Robinson to commemorate her husband, Joseph Fletcher Robinson (d. 11th August 1903). Joseph had contributed to the restoration of St Andrew's Church and also acted as churchwarden for 21 years. This window bears an inscription and depicts the figures of Our Lady and Child with St John the Divine and St Andrew. The northern window was commissioned by BFR to commemorate his mother, Emily Robinson (d. 14th July 1906). This window also bears an inscription and depicts the Good Shepherd with St Peter and St Paul. BFR died just six months after his mother (21st January 1907) and a further inscription was added to commemorate his memory.

It appears that BFR and ACD attended a service at this church on 26th May 1901 that was led by The Revd R.D. Cooke.

16) The Grand Hotel, Seafront, Torquay (57.3 miles)

From St Andrew's Church, double back to the T-junction between Foredown Road and the A381. Turn left and continue for 100 yards to the crossroads by Park Hill Cross Service Station. Turn right towards Bulleigh, Compton and Marldon. Continue for 3.1 miles to a mini-roundabout situated at the exit to Marldon. At this mini-roundabout, take the first exit and continue for 100 yards. At the next roundabout, take the second exit for Preston Seafront. Continue for 1.8 miles along Preston Down Road, Sandringham Gardens, Upper Headland Park Road and Headland Park Road (during 1920, ACD stayed at 5

Headland Grove, located just off and to the right of Headland Park Road). At the traffic lights, turn left onto Torbay Road and continue for 1.2 miles to another set of traffic lights with signs for the Riviera International Centre, Torre Abbey and Newton Abbot (A380). Turn left into Rathmore Road and continue for 30 yards. Turn left and either park for free on the road behind The Grand Hotel (see Plate 43) or use the pay-and-display car park at Torquay Railway Station (opposite). Non-resident visitors wishing to take refreshments at the hotel are also permitted to use their car parking facilities for free.

The original Torquay Railway Station (now called Torre Railway Station) was opened on 18th December 1848 by South Devon Railway. Thereafter, large numbers of wealthy Londoners were able to travel to Torquay in just six hours by train. On 2nd August 1859, the present Torquay Railway Station was opened by Dartmoor and Torbay Railway to accommodate the ever-rising number of tourists. During the 1860s, several large hotels were constructed, including the Belgrave, Victoria and the Great Western (later renamed The Grand Hotel). Visitors to The

Plate 43. The Grand Hotel as seen from Torquay seafront (circa 1910).

104

Grand Hotel are encouraged to take refreshments at the Compass Bar and Lounge and see its fine Art Deco architecture.

In March 1915, ACD and his second wife, Jean, resided at The Grand Hotel for two weeks. During this visit, ACD delivered a lecture at The Pavilion on the Seafront that was entitled *The Great Battles of the War*. Visitors may also be interested to know that Agatha Christie (née Miller) was born in Torquay on 15th September 1890 and that she was particularly fond of The Grand Hotel. The 'Queen of Crime' wrote some 80 mystery novels during her career and invented the characters of Hercule Poirot and Miss Jane Marple. On 24th December 1914, Agatha married Colonel Archibald Christie and the newly-weds spent their honeymoon at The Grand Hotel. The couple divorced on 20th April 1928 and Agatha remarried an archaeologist, Sir Max Mallowan, on 11th September 1930. Lady Mallowan (or Dame Agatha Christie) died aged 85 years, on 12th January 1976, at Cholsey in Oxfordshire.

17) Pavilion Shopping Centre, Vaughan Road, Torquay (58.1 miles)

From The Grand Hotel, double back towards the traffic lights on Torbay Road opposite the Seafront. Turn left and then continue for 0.8 of a mile towards the Harbour. At the first mini-roundabout take the second exit for Marina Pavilion. Visitors can use the Marina and Pavilion Car Park next to the Pavilion Shopping Centre (a small fee is charged for parking).

The Pavilion (see Plate 44) was opened in August 1912 as an entertainment venue. It was designed by Major Henry A. Garrett and built by R.E. Narracott, and combines Classical and Art Nouveau styles. The façade was decorated with Doulton's Carrara enamelled stoneware to create a white palatial effect. The central copper-covered dome is topped with a full-size figure of Britannia, a symbol of patriotism and imperialism. The auditorium featured

Plate 44. The Pavilion in Torquay (circa 1920).

oak panelling, moulded plasterwork and a curved balcony. The Pavilion was reopened in 1987 as a shopping centre.

During July 1914, ACD returned from a tour of North America. Shortly thereafter, WWI began when Austria and Hungary declared war on Serbia. The following month, ACD founded a volunteer home guard unit at Crowborough and started writing regularly about the war for *The Daily Chronicle*.

On September 2nd 1914, ACD was invited to attend a meeting by Charles Masterman MP, who was head of the War Propaganda Bureau. ACD, H.G. Wells, G.K. Chesterton, Thomas Hardy, Rudyard Kipling and other leading British writers were recruited by Masterman to promote the British war effort through their writing. On 30th September 1914, ACD published a recruiting pamphlet for the armed forces entitled *To Arms!* In December 1914, ACD had the first of many articles about the war published by *The Strand Magazine*. This serialisation was later republished

106

as a six-volume history entitled *The British Campaign in France and Flanders*. As has been noted, in February 1915, ACD commenced a tour of at least six British towns and cities to deliver a speech on *The Great Battles of the War*. The last of these talks was given at The Pavilion in Torquay on 27th March 1915. He later returned, on 21st February 1923, to deliver a lecture entitled *The New Revelation*.

18) Torquay Town Hall, Castle Circus, Torquay (59.2 miles)

From the Marina Car Park, return to the mini-roundabout and double back towards The Grand Hotel. After 0.4 of a mile turn right into Belgrave Road and continue past the Victoria Hotel (where ACD resided on 20th February 1923) and then take the second turning on the right (signposted Lucius Street and Post Office). Continue along Tor Church Road and past The Majestic Templestowe Hotel (where the first Lady Conan Doyle and her mother stayed in March 1901). At the crossroads, continue along Tor Hill Road and take the first left into Morgan Avenue. Park for free in the bays located on the right. Walk to the junction of Tor Hill Road with Morgan Avenue and immediately cross the road. Walk 100 yards in the direction of the tall clock tower that belongs to Torquay Town Hall (see Plate 45). Visitors can enter the reception area and request a free tour of the building.

The Town Hall was opened in August 1913, just 12 months after The Pavilion. The building is English renaissance in style and the clock tower above the main entrance rises to a height of 200 feet. The building is constructed from stone and marble supplied by various local quarries, including one at Ipplepen. The Grand Hall on the second floor is capable of seating 1,200 guests with an additional 300 in the gallery. It was in this room during August 1920 that ACD delivered his lecture *Death and the Hereafter*. This meeting was presided over by one Henry Paul Rabbich, the then President of Paignton Spiritualist Society and

Plate 45. The Town Hall in Torquay (circa 1920).

Vice-President of the Southern Counties Union of Spiritualists. ACD stayed with Rabbich at his home, 'The Kraal', at 5 Headland Grove, Preston, Paignton. It is not known whether Lady Conan Doyle accompanied ACD on this occasion.

During 1894, ACD became a life-long member of The Society for Psychical Research. In November 1916, he publically declared his conversion to Spiritualism in an article entitled *A New Revelation. Spiritualism and Religion* that was published by the psychic magazine *Light*. During 1918, ACD expanded upon his beliefs in a book entitled *The New Revelation*. Shortly thereafter, ACD's eldest son, Captain 'Kingsley' Conan Doyle and younger brother, Brigadier-General 'Innes' Doyle, both died from post-war pneumonia. Nevertheless, ACD's faith remained intact and he continued to promote Spiritualism for the rest of his life.

Selected Bibliography

Whilst every effort has been made to follow conventions for the presentation of sources, it has not always proved possible. For example, the authors have consulted birth, marriage, death and English Census records for the three subjects of Chapters 1–3. They have also examined the Last Will and Testaments of ACD, GTB, BFR, Gladys Robinson (BFR's wife), Sir John Robinson (BFR's uncle), Henry Baskerville, Richard Cabell and others. Such records do not readily lend themselves to listing and, in any case, all are available from Ancestry.com or the General Register Office. In other cases, some nineteenth-century texts do not list the name of the author or authors and provide only partial details about the publisher. For these reasons, the authors have either omitted partial entries from this Selected Bibliography, or listed them with explanatory notes in square brackets. They have also elected to omit references to some on-line resources used when researching Chapter 4. This decision was taken in order to preserve clarity and conserve space, and because many websites are, of their nature, transient.

Andrews, C., 'The Bound of the Astorbilts', *The Bookman*, Vol. 15, No. 4, June 1902, (New York: Dodd, Mead & Co.).

Anon., 'A Devon Coachman Whose Name Has Become Immortal', *The Western Times and Gazette*, 1st November 1957 [article about Henry Baskerville].

Anon., 'Ashburton Funeral – The Late Mrs. A. Baskerville', *Mid-Devon Advertiser*, 2nd June 1951 [article about Alice Baskerville, the wife of Henry Baskerville].

Anon., 'Bank-holiday in the West', *The Western Morning News*, 28th May 1901.

Anon., 'Baskerville is Dead – Conan Doyle Used His Name for Sherlock Holmes Story', *The New York Times*, 2nd April 1962.

Anon., 'Beyond the Veil – Sir Arthur Conan Doyle on Modern Miracles', *The Western Morning News*, 5th August 1920 [article about ACD's lecture at Exeter Hippodrome].

Anon., 'B.F.R.', *Daily Express*, 22nd January 1907 [obituary].

Anon., 'Coachman was in at Birth of Baskerville Tale', *Western Evening Herald*, 29th March 1962 [Henry Baskerville obituary].

Anon., 'Congo Wrongs – Sir A. Conan Doyle and Mr. Morel at Plymouth', *The Western Morning News*, 19th November 1909 [article about ACD's first lecture at Plymouth Guildhall].

Anon., 'Council of Legal Education', *The Times*, 15th April 1896 [article reporting that BFR had passed the examination for the Bar at the Inner Temple].

Anon., 'Court Circular', *The Times*, 25th October 1902 [article reporting that King Edward VII had knighted ACD].

Anon., 'Dartmoor in Story', *The Western Morning News*, 2nd March 1931.

Anon., ' "Death and the Hereafter" – Sir Arthur Conan Doyle Lectures at Torquay', *The Torquay Directory and South Devon Journal*, 11th August 1920 [article about ACD's lecture at Torquay Town Hall].

Anon., 'Death of Mr. B. F. Robinson', *Mid-Devon and Newton Times*, 26th January 1907.

Anon., 'Death of Mr. B. F. Robinson', *Vanity Fair*, January 1907.

Anon., 'Doctor Who Helped to Cure the City', *Bristol Evening Post*, 11th April 2006 [article about Dr William Budd, the father of GTB].

Anon., 'Do Fairies Exist? – Sir A. Conan Doyle's Belief – Manifestations in Devon & Cornwall', *The Western Morning News and Mercury*, 24th February 1923.

Anon., *Edinburgh Wanderers Football Club Centenary 1868 – 1968*, (Self-published: 1968).

Anon., 'Festival Sports at Forde Park School', *Mid-Devon Advertiser*, 14th June 1951.

Anon., 'Football. Blackheath v. West Kent', *The Times*, 29th September 1879.

Anon., 'Football. Glasgow Academicals v. Blackheath', *The Times*, 7th March 1878.

Anon., 'Football. Rugby Union Rules. London, Western, and Midland Counties v. Oxford and Cambridge', *The Times*, 10th November 1892.

Anon., 'Football. Rugby Union Rules. London, Western, and Midland Counties v. Oxford and Cambridge', *The Times*, 9th November 1893.

Anon., 'Football. Rugby Union Rules. Oxford v. Cambridge', *The Times*, 17th December 1891.

Anon., 'Football. Rugby Union Rules. Oxford v. Cambridge', *The Times*, 15th December 1892.

Anon., 'Football. Rugby Union Rules. Oxford v. Cambridge', *The Times*, 14th December 1893.

Anon., 'Golden Wedding Celebration – Ashburton Couple', *Western Evening Herald*, 21st November 1944 [article about Henry and Alice Baskerville].

Anon., 'Greatest Delusion or Greatest Fact? – Spiritualists' Claim – Sir A. Conan Doyle at Plymouth', *The Western Morning News and Mercury*, 24th February 1923 [article about ACD's second and final lecture at Plymouth Guildhall].

Anon., 'Henley Royal Regatta', *The Times*, 6th July 1892.

Anon., 'Henley Royal Regatta', *The Times*, 7th July 1892.

Anon., 'Henley Royal Regatta', *The Times*, 8th July 1892.

Anon., 'His Name has Gone Down in Mystery – Harry Baskerville', *South Devon Journal*, 17th October 1951.

Anon., '"Hound of the Baskervilles" – Harry Baskerville Dead; Conan Doyle Used Name', *New York Herald Tribune*, 2nd April 1962.

Anon., 'In Memoriam', *The World*, 22nd January 1907 [BFR obituary].

Anon., *Ipplepen Cricket Club 1890 – 1990*, (Self-published: 1990).

Anon., 'Late Mr. B. Fletcher Robinson – Funeral at Ipplepen', *The Western Morning News*, 25th January 1907.

Anon., 'Life After Death – Sir A. Conan Doyle on Danger of Self-Satisfied', *The Western Morning News*, 6th August 1920 [article about ACD's lecture at Torquay Town Hall].

Anon., 'Linked to the Hound of the Baskervilles', *Dawlish Post*, 15th November 1991 [article about Park Hill House].

Anon., 'London Editor's Death – Mr. B. Fletcher Robinson Succumbs to Typhoid Fever', *The Western Guardian*, 24th January 1907.

Anon., 'Lord Roberts and "The Pilgrims"', *The Times*, 20th June 1904.

Anon., 'Marriages – Robinson:Morris', *The Times*, 5th June 1902.

Anon., 'Mr. Baskerville Returned to see Old Village Friends', *The South Devon Journal*, 13th June 1951.

Anon., 'Mr. Fletcher Robinson – Memorial Service at St. Clement Danes', *Daily Express*, 27th January 1907.

Anon., 'Mystery of the Stonehouse Wall Plaque', *Waterfront News*, Winter 1994.

Anon., 'Obituary – Mr. B. Fletcher Robinson', *The Times*, 22nd January 1907.

Anon., 'Obituary – Mr. Phil Morris, A.R.A.', *The Times*, 24th April 1902.

Anon., 'Obituary – Sir John R. Robinson', *The Times*, 2nd December 1903.

Anon., 'Presentation at Dartmoor Prison', *The Western Morning News*, 31st May 1901.

Anon., 'Rowing. The University Boat Race', *The Times*, 12th February 1894 [article revealing that BFR was selected to row for the Cambridge 'Trial Eight'].

Anon., 'Sidelights on Great Crime Stories (No 10) – 'Ghost Hound' of the Marshes – Was it the Inspiration of Conan Doyle's Story?', *The Evening News*, 25th May 1939.

Anon., 'Sir A. Conan Doyle – Special Interview at Torquay – Spiritualists View of Religion', *The Western Morning News and Mercury*, 21st February 1923.

Anon., 'Sir Arthur Conan Doyle at Torquay', *The Western Morning News*, 29th March 1915 [article about ACD's first lecture at The Pavilion in Torquay].

Anon., 'Some Gossip of the Week', *The Sphere*, 26th January 1907 [BFR obituary].

Anon., 'Spiritualism – New Town Hall, Torquay', *The Torquay Directory and South Devon Journal*, 21st July 1920 [advertisement promoting ACD's forthcoming lecture].

Anon., *The British Medical Journal*, 16th March 1889 [GTB obituary].

Anon., 'The Coronation Honours', *The Times*, 26th June 1902 [article reporting that King Edward VII knighted ACD].

Anon., 'The Escape of Convicts', *The Times*, 17th June 1901.

Anon., *The New Forest Church of All Saints Minstead*, (Minstead Parish Church Council: 1999).

Anon., ' "The New Revelation" – Sir A. Conan Doyle's Lecture at Torquay', *The Western Morning News and Mercury*, 22nd February 1923 [article about ACD's second and final lecture at The Pavilion in Torquay].

Anon., ' "The New Revelation" – Sir Arthur Conan Doyle at Torquay – Life After Death', *Torquay Times*, 23rd February 1923.

Anon., ' "The New Revelation" – Visit of Sir Arthur Conan Doyle to Torquay', *The Torquay Directory and South Devon Journal*, 28th February 1923.

Anon., 'The New Sherlock Holmes Story', *The Bookman*, October 1901, (New York: Dodd, Mead & Co.).

Anon., 'The Original Baskerville Dies, Aged 91', *The Western Morning News*, 30th March 1962.

Anon., 'University Intelligence', *The Times*, 26th November 1897 [article reporting that BFR had been awarded an M.A. degree by his Alma Mater].

Anon., 'When Conan Doyle Practised Medicine in Plymouth', *The Western Morning News*, 2nd February 1949 [article providing a brief overview of ACD's major associations with Devon].

Anon., 'Where Sir Arthur Played Billiards', *Dawlish Post*, n.d. [article about Park Hill House].

Austin, B., 'Dartmoor Revisited or Discoveries in Dartmoor', *Austin's Sherlockian Studies – The Collected Annuals*, (New York: Magico Magazine, 1986) [article about Richard Cabell III and the Baskerville legend].

Bainbridge, J., *Newton Abbot: A History and Celebration of the Town*, (Teffont, Salisbury: Frith, 2004).

Bamberg, R.W., *Haunted Dartmoor – A Ghost-Hunter's Guide*, (Newton Abbot: Peninsula Press, 1993).

Barber C., *Princetown of Yesteryear*, Vols. I & II, (Exeter: Obelisk, 1995).

Barber, S. & C., *Dark and Dastardly Dartmoor*, (Exeter: Obelisk, 1988).

Baring-Gould, S., *A Book of Dartmoor*, (London: Methuen, 1900).

Baring-Gould, S., 'First Report of the Dartmoor Exploration Committee: The Exploration of Grimspound', *Report and Transactions of the Devonshire Association for the Advancement of Science*, Vol. 26, (Devon: The Devonshire Association, 1894).

Baskerville, H.M., 'A letter to the Editor [Noel Vinson]', *The Western Morning News*, 16th February 1949. [This letter, dated 9th February 1949, refers to trips that Baskerville made to Dartmoor with BFR and ACD in 1901.]

Bath, E.J., *Newton Abbot Roundabout*, (Self-published: 1984) [Newton Abbot Public Library].

Bigelow, S.T., 'The Singular Case of Fletcher Robinson' in Ruber, P. (ed.), *The Baker Street Gasogene – a Sherlockian Quarterly*, Vol. 1, No. 2, (New York: 1961). [In 1993, this article was republished by Toronto Reference Library in *The Baker Street Briefs*.]

Bond, Pearce & Co. Solicitors, *Indenture between Benjamin Butland of Leigham Barton, Eggbuckland, farmer and landlord, and George Budd of East Stonehouse, surgeon and tenant,* 16th November 1881. [This item is held by Plymouth & West Devon Record Office: Accession No. '917/35'.]

Bradshaw's General Railway and Steam Navigation Guide, May & June 1901. [This was the most complete of the numerous monthly British railway guides and timetables for this period and is held at The National Archive in Richmond: Ref. 'Rail 903/118'.]

Brandenburg, B., Doyle, A.C., Green, A.K., Poe, E.A., Robinson, B.F. & Stevenson, R.L., (Patten, W., ed.), *Great Short Stories: Volume 1 Detective Stories,* (New York: P.F. Collier & Son, 1906). [This anthology of twelve short stories includes both *The Sign of Four* and *A Scandal in Bohemia* by ACD and also *The Vanished Millionaire* by BFR.]

Bristol & Clifton Directory, (Bristol: J. Wright & Co., 1880 & 1886).

Budd, A.J. et al., (Marshall, F., ed.), *Football: The Rugby Union Game,* (London: Cassell & Co. Ltd, 1892).

Byng, B., *Dartmoor's Mysterious Megaliths,* (Plymouth: Baron Jay, n.d.).

Carr, J.D., *The Life of Sir Arthur Conan Doyle,* (London: John Murray, 1949).

Carter, P., *Newton Abbot,* (Exeter: The Mint Press, 2004).

Cassell's Family Magazine, (Pemberton, M., ed.), (London: Cassell, Petter & Galpin, December 1896 – November 1897). [These include three articles by BFR.]

Cassell's Magazine, (Pemberton, M., ed.), (London: Cassell & Co. Ltd, December 1897 – December 1903). [These include twenty-one articles, four short stories and two poems by BFR.]

The Chanticleer, (Foakes-Jackson, J., ed. & others), (Cambridge: J. Palmer, 1890–1894) [Jesus College magazine that changed its name to *The Chanticlere* from October 1892].

Chapman, L., *The Ancient Dwellings of Grimspound and Hound Tor,* (Chudleigh: Orchard Publications, 1996).

The Cheltonian, June 1901 [report about a cricket match played on 7th–8th June between Cheltenham College and an Incogniti touring-team that featured ACD].

Clifton College Register 1862–1947, 47th edn, (Old Cliftonian Society, 1947).

Climatological Returns for Ashburton, Druid, Devon, May & June 1901. [Daily weather observation form prepared for the Royal Meteorological Society by one Fabyn Amery and held by the Met Office National Meteorological Archive, Exeter: Ref. '910070'.]

Climatological Returns for Great Yarmouth, Norfolk, April 1901. [Daily weather observation form prepared for the Royal Meteorological Society and held by the Met Office National Meteorological Archive, Exeter: Ref. '910741'.]

Climatological Returns for Princetown, Devon, May & June 1901. [Daily weather observation form prepared for the Royal Meteorological Society by Dartmoor Prison staff and held by the Met Office National Meteorological Archive, Exeter: Ref. '911426'.]

Cooke, H.R., 'A letter to the Editor [Noel Vinson]', *The Western Morning News*, 14th February 1949. [This letter, dated 7th February 1949, refers to a trip that Cooke's father and BFR made to Dartmoor in 1901.]

Cooke, R.D., *The Churches and Parishes of Ipplepen and Torbryan*, c.1930. [This article appears to have been published as a supplement to *Ipplepen Parish Magazine*.]

Cramer, W.S., 'The Enigmatic B. Fletcher Robinson and the Writing of The Hound of the Baskervilles', in Penzler, O. (ed.), *The Armchair Detective*, Vol. 26, No. 4, (New York: The Mysterious Press, Autumn 1991).

Crossing, W., *Princetown – Its Rise and Progress*, (Brixham, Devon: Quay Publications, 1989).

Daily Express, May 1900 – June 1904, (London: C. Arthur Pearson Ltd). [These include one hundred and two by-lined articles, one poem and one playlet by BFR.]

Dam, H.J.W., 'Arthur Conan Doyle: An Appreciation of the

Author of "Sir Nigel", the Great Romance Which Begins Next Sunday', *New York Tribune Sunday Magazine*, 26th November 1905.

Djabri, S.C., *The Story of the Sepulchre – The Cabells of Buckfastleigh and the Conan Doyle Connection,* (London: Shamrock Press, 1989).

Doidge's Western Counties Yearbook, (Plymouth: 1879–80).

Doyle, A.C., 'The Adventure of the Norwood Builder, *Collier's Weekly Magazine,* (New York: P.F. Collier & Son, October 1903.).

Doyle, A.C., 'Dry Plates on a Wet Moor', *The Hound,* Vol. 3, (Fareham: Sherlock Publications, 1994). [Originally published in *The British Journal of Photography,* November 1882.]

Doyle, A.C., *The Hound of the Baskervilles,* (London: George Newnes, 1902).

Doyle, A.C., *The Lost World,* (London: Hodder & Stoughton, 1912).

Doyle, A.C., *Memories and Adventures,* (London: Greenhill Books, 1988) [facsimile of edition published London: Hodder & Stoughton, 1924].

Doyle, A.C., 'My First Experiences in Practice', *The Strand Magazine,* Vol. 66, No. 395, (London: George Newnes, November 1923).

Doyle, A.C., *The Stark Munro Letters,* (London: Longmans, Green & Co., 1895).

Dunnill, M., *Dr. William Budd. Bristol's Most Famous Physician,* (Bristol: Redcliffe Press, 2006).

Edwards, O.D., *The Quest for Sherlock Holmes,* (Edinburgh: Mainstream Publishing, 1983).

Elvins, J.W., *Plymouth Street Directory,* (Plymouth: 1867 & 1873).

Evans, P., 'The Mystery of Baskerville', *Daily Express,* 16th March 1959.

Eyre Brothers' Plymouth, Devonport and Stonehouse Street Directory, (London: Eyre Bros., 1880–1890).

Fraser, J.M., & Robinson, B.F., 'Fog Bound' in Sisley, C. (ed.),

The London Magazine, (London: Amalgamated Press, August 1903) [a short story].

Fraser, J.M., & Robinson, B.F., 'The Trail of the Dead – The Strange Experience of Dr. Robert Harland' in Hutchinson, A. (ed.), *The Windsor Magazine,* (London: Ward & Lock, December 1902 – May 1903) [serialised story in six parts].

French, A., *Ipplepen,* (Exeter: Obelisk, 2003).

Gilbert, T., 'A Letter to The Royal College of Physicians of London', (Unpublished, 17th May 1882). [Thomas Gilbert was the 'Clerk to the University' of Edinburgh and his brief letter reads: 'I hereby certify that Mr Arthur Conan Doyle commenced the study of medicine on 1st November 1877 and graduated as M.B. and C.M. of this University on 1st August 1881.' This statement is significant in that it contradicts the accepted opinion that ACD commenced his medical studies during October 1886. This letter is still held by the library of The Royal College of Physicians: Ref. 'G49 of the ALS (historic letter) collection'.]

Goodall, E.W., *William Budd, M.D. Edin., F.R.S. – The Bristol Physician and Epidemiologist,* (London: Arrowsmith, 1936).

Gore's Directory for Liverpool and its Environs, (Liverpool: J. Mawdsley & Son, 1845–1867).

The Granta, (Lehmann, R.C., ed. & others), (Cambridge: W.P. Spalding, 1892–97). [These include sixteen poems, one song and one playlet by BFR.]

Green, R.L., 'Bertram Fletcher Robinson: An Old and Valued Friend – The Adventure of the Two Collaborators' in Purves S. (ed.), *Hound and Horse, A Dartmoor Commonplace Book,* (London: The Sherlock Holmes Society of London, 1992).

Green, R.L., 'Conan Doyle and his Cricket' in Black, M.C. (ed.), *The Victorian Cricket Match – The Sherlock Holmes Society of London versus the P.G. Wodehouse Society,* (London: The Sherlock Holmes Society of London, 2001).

Green, R.L., 'The Hound of the Baskervilles, Part 1', *The Journal of the Sherlock Holmes Society of London,* Vol. 25, No. 3,

(London: Sherlock Holmes Society, 2001).

Green, R.L., 'The Hound of the Baskervilles, Part 2', *The Journal of the Sherlock Holmes Society of London*, Vol. 25, No. 4, (London: Sherlock Holmes Society, 2002).

Hammond, D., *The Club: Life and Times of Blackheath F. C.,* (London: MacAitch, 1999).

Hands, S. & Webb, P., *The Book of Ashburton – Pictorial History of a Dartmoor Stannary Town,* (Tiverton: Halsgrove House, 2004).

James, T., *About Princetown,* (Chudleigh: Orchard Publications, 2002).

Jones, K.I., *The Mythology of The Hound of the Baskervilles,* 2nd edn, (Penzance: Oakmagic Publications, 1996).

Kelly's Directory of Devonshire, (London: Kelly's Directories Ltd, 1878/79 & 1910) [Ipplepen entries].

Klinefelter, W., *Origins of Sherlock Holmes,* (Bloomington, Indiana: Gaslight Publications, 1983).

Lellenberg, J., Stashower, D. & Foley, C., *Arthur Conan Doyle: A Life in Letters,* (London: HarperPress, 2007).

Lethbridge, H.J., *Torquay & Paignton: The Making of a Modern Resort,* (Chichester: Phillimore & Co., 2003).

London and Provincial Medical Directory, (London: John Churchill, 1848–69).

London Medical Directory, (London: C. Mitchell, 1845).

Lycett, A., *Conan Doyle: The Man Who Created Sherlock Holmes,* (London: Weidenfeld & Nicolson, 2007).

Mann, R., *Buckfast & Buckfastleigh,* (Exeter: Obelisk, 1994).

Marshall, A., *Out and About: Random Reminiscences,* (London: John Murray, 1933).

Marshall, F. (ed.), *Football: The Rugby Union Game,* (London: Cassell & Co. Ltd, 1892) [includes article by Arthur Budd].

Marshall, H.P. (with Jordan, J.P.), *Oxford v. Cambridge: The Story of the University Rugby Match,* (London: Clerke & Cockeran, 1951).

Marshall's Street Directory for Clifton, Bristol, (1842–75).

Mathews' Annual Bristol & Clifton Directory & Almanack, (Bristol: Matthew Mathews, 1850–1869).

Mathews' Bristol Directory, (Bristol: J. Wright & Co., 1870–1879).

Matson, C.G., 'Automobile Topics: The Paris Automobile Show', *The World*, 11th December 1906. [BFR was editor of this newspaper at the time of his death. According to various sources he contracted typhoid whilst visiting the Paris Automobile Show during December 1906.]

Matson, C.G., 'Automobile Topics: The Paris Automobile Show', *The World,* 18th December 1906.

Matson, C.G., 'Automobile Topics: The Paris Automobile Show', *The World,* 25th December 1906.

Maurice, A.B., 'Conan Doyle's "The Hound of the Baskervilles" ', *The Bookman*, (New York: Dodd, Mead & Co., May 1902).

McClure, M.W., 'Myth-Conception Regarding The Hound of the Baskervilles', *The Devonshire Chronicle: The Quarterly Journal of The Chester Baskerville Society*, Vol. 1, No. 2, (Illinois: The Chester Baskerville Society, 1989).

McNabb, J., 'The Curious Incident of the Hound on Dartmoor' *Occasional Papers, No. 1 – Bootmakers of Toronto*, (Toronto: Bootmakers of Toronto, 1984).

Medical Directory, 1870–1905, (London: Churchill Livingstone).

Michelmore, H.G., 'A letter to the Editor [Noel Vinson]', *The Western Morning News*, 1949. [This letter, dated 2nd February 1949, was written in response to comments made by J. Dickson Carr in *The Life of Sir Arthur Conan Doyle*, about BFR's involvement with *The Hound of the Baskervilles*.]

Michelmore, H.G., *Fishing Facts and Fancies*, (Exeter: A. Wheaton & Co., 1946).

Michelmore, H.G., '*Letter to Miss Mary Taylor*', (Unpublished: 30th January 1907). [This letter records Michelmore's reaction to BFR's death and is held by the British Library of Political and Economic Science, London: Ref. 'Mill-Taylor, Vol. 29, No. 307'.]

The Newtonian, (Newton Abbot: G.H. Hearder, 1881–1890) [the magazine of Newton Abbot Proprietary College, edited by BFR between 1887 and 1889].

Oswald, N.C., 'The Budds of North Tawton: A Medical Family of the 19th Century', *Report and Transactions of the Devonshire Association for the Advancement of Science*, Vol. 117, (Torquay: Devonshire Press, 1985).

Pearce, D.N., 'The Illness of Dr. George Turnavine Budd and its Influence on the Literary Career of Sir Arthur Conan Doyle', *Journal of Medical Biography*, Vol. 3, No. 4, (London: Royal Society of Medicine Press, 1995).

Pearson, H., *Conan Doyle, his Life and Art,* (London: Macdonald and Jane's, 1977).

Pearson's Magazine, (London: C. Arthur Pearson Ltd, March 1900 – December 1904). [These include fifteen articles, two short stories and two poems by BFR.]

Pemberton, M., *Sixty Years Ago and After*, (London: Hutchinson & Co., 1936).

Pemberton, M., *Wheels of Anarchy*, (London: Cassell & Co. Ltd, 1908).

Pugh, B.W., *A Chronology of the Life of Sir Arthur Conan Doyle – New Revised and Expanded Edition,* (Self-published: 2003).

Pugh, B.W., *A Monograph on George Turnavine Budd,* (Self-published: 2008).

Rice, F.A. (compiler), *The Granta and its Contributors 1889–1914,* (London: Constable & Co. Ltd, 1924).

Robinson, B.F. et al., (Hutchinson, A., ed.), 'Chronicles in Cartoon: A Record of our Own Times', *The Windsor Magazine*, (London: Ward & Lock, December 1905 – November 1906) [twelve illustrated articles about notable individuals who were featured in *Vanity Fair*].

Robinson, B.F., 'The Chronicles of Addington Peace', *The Lady's Home Magazine of Fiction*, (London: C. Arthur Pearson Ltd, August 1904 – January 1905) [six short stories].

Robinson, B.F., 'The Fortress of the First Britons. A Description of the Fortress of Grimspound on Dartmoor', *Pearson's Magazine*, Vol. 28, (London: C. Arthur Pearson Ltd, September 1904).

Robinson, B.F., 'How Mr. Denis O'Halloran Transgressed his Code', *Appleton's Magazine*, Vol. 9, No. 1, (New York: D. Appleton & Co., January 1907). [This was the last short story that BFR wrote.]

Robinson, B.F., *John Bull's Store,* (London: Elkin & Co., 1904), [a tax tariff reform anthem: music by Robert Eden (1903), lyrics by BFR].

Robinson, B.F., *The Little Loafer*, (London: Elkin & Co., 1904), [a tax tariff reform anthem: music by Robert Eden, lyrics by BFR].

Robinson, B.F., 'People Much Talked About in London', *Munsey's Magazine*, Vol. 37, No. 2, (New York: Frank A. Munsey, May 1907).

Robinson, B.F., (Pemberton, M., ed.), *Rugby Football*, (London: A. D. Innes & Co., 1896).

Robinson, B.F., (Savory, E.W., ed.), *Sporting Pictures,* (London: Cassell & Co. Ltd, 1902).

Robinson, J.R., *Fifty Years on Fleet Street*, (London: Macmillan & Co., 1904).

Rodin, A.E., & Key, J.D., 'A Plymouth Adventure: Arthur Conan Doyle and George Turnavine Budd', *Baker Street Miscellanea*, No. 57, (Chicago, Illinois: The Socialist Press, 1989).

Rodin, A.E., & Key, J.D., *Medical Casebook of Doctor Arthur Conan Doyle,* (Malabar, Florida: Krieger Publishing, 1964).

Ruber, P.A., 'Sir Arthur Conan Doyle & Fletcher Robinson: an Epitaph', *The Baker Street Gasogene*, Vol. 1, No. 2, (New York: 1961).

Saville, G., 'The War of the Baskervilles', *The Independent*, 11th July 2001.

Selleck, D., *Backalong in Plymouth Town: Stories from West Country History – 1780–1880*, No. 1, (Redruth: Dyllansow Truran, 1984).

Selleck, D., 'Dr. Budd, Bully or Benefactor', *Western Evening*

Herald, 21st July 1990 [article about GTB's uncle, Dr John Wreford Budd].

Selleck, D., 'Tough Talking Cured Patients', *Western Evening Herald*, 16th August 1983 [article about GTB's uncle, Dr John Wreford Budd].

The Shirburnian, June 1901 [report about a cricket match played on 3rd–4th June between Sherborne School and an Incogniti touring-team that featured ACD].

Simpson, A.W.B., 'Shooting Felons: Law, Practice, Official Culture and Perceptions of Morality', *Journal of Law and Society*, Vol. 32, No. 2, (Oxford: Blackwell Publishing, June 2005) [a history of convict escapes from HMP Dartmoor].

Spiring, P.R., A *Monograph on Bertram Fletcher Robinson,* (Self-published: 2008).

Stashower, D., *Teller of Tales: The Life of Arthur Conan Doyle,* (New York: Henry Holt & Co., 1999).

Stonehouse Street Directory, 1852–73, (Plymouth: F. Brendon).

Summers, V., 'The Case of Conan Doyle and the Amazing Dr. Budd', *Devon Life Magazine*, June 1990.

The Three Towns Directory for Plymouth, Devonport and Stonehouse, (Plymouth: W.J. Trythall, 1877).

Travis, J., *Lynton and Lynmouth – Glimpses of the Past,* (The Breedon Books Publishing Co., 1997).

Vanity Fair (Robinson, B.F., ed.), (London: Harmsworth, May 1904 – October 1906). [These include twenty-seven articles, thirty-three short stories, two poems, one song and eight playlets by BFR.]

Weller, P.L., 'Deposits in the Vault: Together Again on the Moor?', *Stimson & Company Gazette*, No. 3, (USA: 1992).

Weller, P.L., *The Hound of the Baskervilles – Hunting the Dartmoor Legend,* (Tiverton: Devon Books, 2001).

Wheeler, E., 'The Grand Old School of Newton Abbot', *Mid-Devon Advertiser*, 8th August 1970.

Wheeler, E., '"Rescuer" of Sherlock Holmes', *The Western Morning News,* 24th October 1969.

White, W., *History Gazetteer & Directory of Devonshire*, (Sheffield: Robert Leader, 1850) [entries on Ipplepen].

Will, H., *Ford Park Cemetery, Plymouth – A Heritage Trail*, (Plymouth: Ford Park Cemetery Trust, 2004).

Williams, J.E.H., 'The Reader: Arthur Conan Doyle', *The Bookman*, (London: Hodder & Stoughton, April 1902).

Zunic, J., 'Origins of the Hound, 1: Bertie and Max', *The Northumberland Gazette*, November 1989.

Private documents not in the public domain

Anon., *Blackheath Football Club Records, 1875–1898*, (Unpublished, n.d.) [This club was later renamed Blackheath Rugby Club.]

Howlett, A., (Unpublished lecture-notes: 1976).

McNabb, J., *My Friend, Mr. Fletcher Robinson*, (Unpublished: c. 1985).

Michelmore, H.G., *A letter to Henry Baskerville*, (Unpublished: 8th February 1949). [This is a response to a letter from Baskerville, dated 7th February 1949, that comments upon BFR's involvement with *The Hound of the Baskervilles*.]

Robinson, F., *Reminiscences of Frederick Robinson*, (Unpublished: 1911) [ten thousand words of autobiographical notes written by one of BFR's uncles].

Smyllie, F., *History of Meade-King, Robinson & Co. Ltd*, (Unpublished: n.d.) [extended essay on the development of this company that was founded by BFR's father].

Sutton, M., *The Darling Budds of Devon*, (Unpublished: n.d.).

Reports prepared for Brian Pugh and Paul Spiring

Anon., *George Turnavine Budd*, (Devon Record Office, 2005).

Anon., *Henry Mathews Baskerville*, (Devon Record Office, 2005).

Anon., *Park Hill House in Ipplepen*, (Devon Record Office, 2005).

Anon., *Squire Richard Cabell III*, (Devon Record Office, 2005).

Beckwith, J., *Arthur Budd*, (The Royal College of Physicians of London, 2006).

Duncan, S., *BFR and The Isthmian Library*, (British Library, 2006).

Duncan, S., *The London Residences of BFR*, (British Library, 2005).

Ferguson, I., *Dr. Arthur Conan Doyle*, (Edinburgh University, 2007).

Ferguson, I., *Dr. George Turnavine Budd*, (Edinburgh University, 2007).

Gillies, S., Articles by-lined by BFR and published in the *Daily Express*, April 1900 – July 1904, (British Library, 2005–2006) [a series of seventeen items].

Willmoth., F., *BFR and Dr. Henry Menzies,* (Jesus College, The University of Cambridge, 2005).

Internet sources
Casey, P., *Clifton Rugby Football Club History*, at: www.cliftonrfchistory.co.uk

Pugh, B.W., The Conan Doyle (Crowborough) Establishment, at: www.the-conan-doyle-crowborough-establishment.com

Spiring, P.R., *Bertram Fletcher Robinson*, at: www.bfronline.biz